*"As you accompany Melissa on her journey,
you will discover the joy that is available to those
who have chosen to be held by Jesus."*

I'm so excited that Melissa finally put pen to paper and wrote her story. Never have you heard such a real and raw story about God's grace and what it really means to be held by Him. What a great read!

—**SARAH WORMAN-CONNELL**, CHOREOGRAPHER

Held is such a picture of the way Jesus steps into the hardest and messiest parts of our lives and comforts us in a way that only He can. Melissa has a way of drawing you into her story in such a relatable and authentic way. If you are seeking more than inspiration, but how God can transform what was meant for destruction into a beautiful story, then keep reading! I believe God will show you what it means to be *Held*, too!

—**TIFFANY JOHNSON**, SPEAKER, AUTHOR,
SHARK ATTACK SURVIVOR AND AMPUTEE

If you are in a place of pain or discouragement today, you need to read Melissa Eadie's story. Her battle with cancer and the eventual amputation of her leg at a young age are tragic when viewed without the eyes of faith. However, as you accompany Melissa on her journey, you will discover the joy that is available to those who have chosen to be held by Jesus. Melissa's book, *Held*, tells a vibrant story and turns our hearts to the God who is always good. Melissa's story will convince you that you are never alone even at the darkest hour in life.

—**CAROL MCLEOD**, BESTSELLING AUTHOR AND SPEAKER

Held is a very personal and raw story of God's leading through the toughest of trials. Melissa Eadie shares her vulnerable life experiences from the dismay of a young woman about to lose her leg, to the realities of life after the amputation. The most impactful thread through the entire book is how she never lost sight of Almighty God, trusted in Him, and allowed Him to lead even during the darkest of times. This book will resonate with anyone who has been through (or is going through) a life challenge. You will be encouraged to get up and live the life that God has for you.

—**DR. PAULA MCDONALD**, AUTHOR, SPEAKER, WELLNESS
EXPERT IN THE INTEGRATION OF SCIENCE AND THE BIBLE

HELD

HELD

MELISSA EADIE

BRIDGE
LOGOS

Newberry, FL 32669

Bridge-Logos
Newberry, FL 32669

HELD:
A Memoir from Cancer Survivor and Amputee Melissa Eadie
by Melissa Eadie

Library of Congress Catalog Card Number: 2021936159

International Standard Book Number: 978-1-61036-265-8

International Standard Book Number eBook: 978-0-7684-6190-9

International Standard Book Number Hardcover: 978-0-7684-6191-6

International Standard Book Number Large Print: 978-0-7684-6192-3

Edited by Lynn Copeland

Cover/Interior design by Kent Jensen | knail.com

Cover photo by Casi Scanlon, Casi Elizabeth Photo | casielizabethphoto.com

To my mom—

my best friend, confidante, and someone I aspire to be like.

One day I hope that I can touch as many lives as you have.

You are the sincerest reflection of the Proverbs 31 woman.

CONTENTS

FOREWORD

Sometimes in life, we are blessed enough to cross paths with an extraordinary human being, a rare soul—the kind of person who exhales beauty into a broken world. Melissa Eadie is one of God's gifts to me. It's been my joy to come alongside of her in different seasons of her life. She has taught me what it looks like to live with grace in the midst of adversity. She has shown me what it looks like to live with courage in the midst of great loss. And she has tutored me in what it looks like to live with kindness in the midst of difficult circumstances. She has a profound sense of God's mercy and His grace that walk with us through grief and allow us to process our emotions in His presence.

When I asked during an interview how cancer and the loss of her leg had changed her, she shared this:

> I felt like God sent me to LA to go to this amazing school and be a light to people. I don't know if people would've seen me the same way if I came to LA with all of my limbs and was just a super-friendly girl who loved Jesus. There's something about when He allows us to go through a loss or trial that grows us. I saw how people said, "You don't have a leg. How can you be so positive?" And I was able to say that it was because I serve a God who is mightier. I was able to give my testimony. Sometimes we grow more in the trials in life than just having an easy-breezy life. Whoever sits in my makeup chair hears my story.

The first time she danced at our church after the loss of her leg, I could barely breathe. She ushers in the presence of God in such a sweet and tangible way. You will sense that in this raw, personal memoir as she shares not only intimate moments of her life, but her faith in an extraordinary God. Her passion for Jesus and love for others is infectious—and cancer didn't take that from her. Whether your scars are visible or not, she will encourage you to allow God to help you first process your pain and then share your story. I'm thrilled that you get to meet this beautiful woman I know and love. You will not only come to love Melissa, too, but you will get to know the God who loves without limits and lets us know what it feels like to be held.

—Angela Donadio
Author, speaker, and host of
the "Make Life Matter" podcast

INTRODUCTION

I was first offered the opportunity to write this book as a nineteen-year-old, by an agent who was ready to get my story into the hands of hurting people. I attempted a few chapters, but eventually decided not to pursue the book at that time. Then, at the ripe age of twenty-four, I was praying that God would use me in ways I couldn't fathom, not wanting another year to pass without me really pursuing His purpose for my life. I mean, with how crazy my life has been, there has to be some purpose for it all...right? I am a firm believer that everything happens for a reason, that not one door closes without another opening, and that all ashes can be made beautiful. So one night I asked Him, *What do You ask of me? Speak to me, and I will do it!* As clear as day, I heard the word "WRITE." That was four years ago!

I'm so thankful for friends and family who never gave up on me completing this book and for their many words of encouragement throughout the years. Even as the book started to form, when I felt defeated and discouraged that my words held no worth, one of my best friends, Cristy, spoke truth and wisdom into me. She reminded me that "there will be bumps and some hard days, but you know how to fight hard journeys. You've already done it many times. Let's get this book done."

Though it took me nine years from concept to completion, God's timing is never flawed. He was aware that, when I was nineteen, I barely knew the half of what He was doing in me and through me. Praise God for His perfect timing and His perfect will. Let me give you a little backstory that has gotten me to where I am today.

"This is what it means to be held." I remember hearing these lyrics, as my friend and choreographer, Sarah Worman-Connell, played the song she had in her heart for me to dance to in an upcoming show. I had just experienced the most significant life change. My heart was grieving, but I had to cling to the only thing I knew that was good and consistent: my God. I was surprised that I had never heard this song by Natalie Grant, as it had been out for a good chunk of time. I remember tears filling my eyes, threatening to flow freely, because the words resounded so profoundly. I had never felt more vulnerable or raw in my entire life, all nineteen years on the planet. I felt like the emotional instability could break me at any moment. But I wasn't sure if I was ready to reveal the brokenness within me to anyone but myself. I wanted to be strong, trying to remember that I served a God who brought beauty from ashes. What the devil meant for evil, God was continuing to work for my good.

He was not left flabbergasted by my current circumstances. He was not shocked at the turn of events. He was not rocked and caught off guard. Even with everything going through my head, He did not share the same fears and anxieties. "This is what it means to be held." After only a month of adjusting to my new life, those words, "to be held," spun around in my head. I tried to envision what dancing would be like without a crucial tool I used to have. I was physically, spiritually, and emotionally in need of being *held*. I repeated the words in my head, connecting myself to them, memorizing and working to understand them. I never realized it would become my anthem, my start to a journey that only a faithful, loving, heavenly Father could assemble. The journey would take years to fully process, but what I would learn along the way I would be unable to keep to myself. I cannot keep silent about what God has accomplished in me, has taught me, and has pressed upon my heart. So, here we go.

This is my story. This is what it means to be held.

CHAPTER ONE

JUST A PULLED MUSCLE

I have always laughed when reading books that start with, "I grew up in such and such town." Yet, I now realize that the only way to start my journey is to go back to the beginning of it all. And of course, it begins with the town I grew up in. So here I am, about to type those words, realizing there is no shame; it just is what it is.

I grew up in Fredericksburg, Virginia, in a house my father built, in a bedroom where I was born (my parents chose to have all home births), with five siblings. Yes, you heard that correctly! I am the middle kid of five, and though I haven't always loved being from a big family, I wish I could tell my younger self, *You're going to love who your siblings turn out to be and your relationships with each of them.*

My father is the most hard-working man I have ever known, and my mom sacrificed many of her dreams to be a stay-at-home mom and homeschool teacher. She will tell you that if she had the choice to do it over, she wouldn't change a thing. My parents raised us to pursue God hard, to show kindness, and not to judge a book by its cover. We attended Saturday services at Ohev Yisrael, a Messianic Jewish congregation, where I met some of my dearest and best friends to this day. I gave my life to Jesus as a five-year-old, sitting on my mom's lap, aching to have what she held so dear. I may have barely been able to recite my ABCs, but I knew I wanted Jesus.

Growing up, my parents allowed each of us kids to pick one activity that we were willing to throw ourselves into entirely. Two of my brothers picked baseball, while my sister and I chose ballet. My youngest brother, Justin, was born with apraxia and suffered from seizures, leaving him with special needs, so he spent most of his time with my mom, painting, singing, and riding his scooter outside. I loved to dance with all that was in me. I was naturally a very shy kid, but there was something about dance that made me feel like a different person. At seven years old, I remember working so hard to get my splits. When I finally achieved it, I was running around the house falling into my splits all the time (my dance instructor, Mrs. Kegg, would cringe if she knew how often I would do this without being stretched). I continued to dance and put my time and energy into building my endurance and flexibility; it was a daily part of me.

My childhood was beautiful. I truly mean it, because even with the hardships my family was dragged through, my parents never failed us kids. They never neglected to provide or to teach us in the way that we should go (Proverbs 22:6). To this day, my dad is a very skilled builder, and he has been the sole provider for our family. In 2002, my Uncle Gary discussed opening a Donut Connection franchise but was unsure if he wanted to go into the business by himself, so my dad offered to be a silent partner. His construction business was doing well and he felt confident that he could make the investment into the new business.

As a little girl, I felt like the donut shop was truly a magical, whimsical place. I remember watching the donuts being decorated and placed in the front of the shop. Seeing the lines going out the door in the morning, and the smiles of so many customers, all made it feel like a fantasy world. Years went on, jokes were made that my dad was the Donut Man, and I always assumed the business was doing well. But it took a lot of donuts to make rent and payroll, and the location did not have adequate visibility. I had no idea that the business was barely staying afloat. Through the years, my parents and my uncle's family tried to make the business work, but it was a constant struggle. However, even with all the burdens my parents carried on their shoulders, they still pushed us kids to pursue our dreams and have goals. They never told us a passion was unacceptable or unrealistic. They supported each and every dream, no matter how often those dreams changed with age.

CHILDHOOD DREAMS

When I was seven, still loving dance, I also wanted to add being a country singer to my dream roster, taking inspiration from Shania Twain. At age eleven, I decided I wanted to put everything into pursuing the career of a prima ballerina. However, at age thirteen, with Disney Channel being a frequent pastime in our household, I wanted to be an actress and work for Disney. I had dreams of being on *High School Musical* or *The Suite Life of Zach and Cody.* And lastly, at age twenty-nine, who would have thought I would still be pursuing that industry, just in a completely different avenue: makeup artistry and special effects (referred to in the industry as "Fx").

When I was age thirteen, my parents did what they could to help me achieve the goal of becoming an actress. I had no idea that my parents were working through a failing business, with bills stacking up, not knowing where the next paycheck would be coming from, with so much of my dad's company's money going into the Donut Connection. I learned in later years that our house, which had once been paid off, had been used for collateral to obtain the business loan to purchase the equipment and renovations for the store. The grim reality was that if the shop didn't land on its feet, we could have potentially lost our home. Despite all the chaos, when an audition opportunity for an agency that worked with Disney Channel came along, my mom got all her ducks in a row and drove me and my best friend, Helena, the two and a half hours to Maryland.

The audition turned out to be a huge success! My quirky fourteen-year-old self made a good impression (braces and all). They let me know that I would be hearing back from them shortly. When they called the next day they said they were very excited to bring me on with the agency, but it didn't come without a cost. These costs included classes and traveling, so even though my parents wanted to help me with this massive dream of mine, they sat down, did the math, and just couldn't swing it. My mom told me that we would have to turn the offer down and wait for God to bring the next opportunity. I was crushed. However, the perks were that I would be able to dance in my studio's production of

The Nutcracker that was just two weeks away. There would have been an audition in New York the same day as the recital. My commitment level may have been slightly flawed, since I was willing to miss a recital in which I had a solo and several other parts that would not have been easy to replace. Dropping out with only two weeks' notice never occurred to me as being a very thoughtless thing to do. Oh, how our young minds work!

The day of *The Nutcracker* rolled around, and the dressing room began to fill with dancers in costume. The atmosphere was thick with both nervousness and excitement. I was getting into my first costume, the Soldier Doll, and my nerves were threatening to consume me. But as the music started, curtains opened, and the show began, I felt only sheer excitement to be there. When my music started, I was ready. With my best doll impression, I moved in a robotic motion with the music. The music began to speed up and as it did so, I kicked my legs up with all the power I had within me. When I did my fouetté combination, I felt the rise of applause. The audience was a kind group of people as I have looked back on the videos, and frankly, my foot was drooping as I spun. I ended my dance feeling exuberant. The rest of the show sped by, with a short lunch break then on to the second show. Before I knew it, the curtains were closing and the set was being taken down.

WHAT A PAIN

The next morning rolled in, and when I got up out of bed, I immediately felt a blistering, sharp pain in my right leg. It was so severe that I couldn't walk, so I called my mom into my room. We both assumed I had pulled a muscle during the Soldier Doll dance because of the amount of kicking it involved. During the next week I babied my leg. Though the pain subsided enough to allow me to walk, it was still a constant nuisance. We proceeded with caution. I wanted to go back to dance, but after a discussion with my instructor, we decided we needed to wait until I was completely healed. My family has always tried to hold off on going to doctors as long as possible because a cold was just a cold, and we just figured a pulled muscle was just a pulled muscle. With only a brief history of my grandmother having skin cancer, and no hereditary diseases, we never felt the need to panic. However, after two months of swelling and pain, we decided it could potentially be more than a pulled muscle and it was time to have it checked out.

The first doctor we visited took an x-ray, which showed a slight shadow, so he sent us to the main hospital in the area for an MRI. From there, we went to Richmond to see an orthopedic doctor, who took another x-ray. He showed us the area that was causing concern and explained that it could be one of three things:

1. It could be an infection.
2. It could be a benign tumor.
3. It could be cancer.

He proceeded to order a biopsy to be done in the next few days. I remember going to youth group that weekend and sharing my experience with a dear friend of mine. I told him that it was probably nothing and that I didn't know why everyone was making such a big deal about it. He looked down at my leg, which I had wrapped in a pathetic ace bandage because the pain was so bad. With concern written all over his face, he said in such a sad voice, "But Melissa…what if it is something more? What if it is cancer?" I honestly didn't know much about cancer, so I just said,

"Well, we will find out in a couple of days and know for sure what is going on. For now, let's not worry."

The next couple of days flew by, and there I was in a cap and gown, lying on a table preparing to have my biopsy. This was my first surgery ever, and I had no idea what to expect. So, with a racing heart, I was told to count backward from ten, and before I knew it, I was waking up in a dark outpatient room. My mom was sitting in the corner of the room. At the time, I didn't make the connection that she never made eye contact with me until the doctor came in. He walked in and said, "Well, we have the results back from the biopsy." He paused and then said with a regretful tone, "We have found that you do have cancer. It is still in the very early stages, so we caught it in time. We will get you in to see a pediatric oncologist."

As I was writing this section of the book, my mom told me that Dr. Foster had come in to speak with her in the waiting room and informed her that they found I had cancer. My mom was trying to be brave; she now knew what we were facing. She listened attentively to what the plan would be, but when he mentioned chemotherapy, she began to tear up. She asked if I would lose my hair, to which he replied, "Yes." She knew that this part of the process would be incredibly hard for me as a fourteen-year-old girl, and it tugged at her heart. I hadn't known this part of the story until now. My mom is incredibly selfless. Her entire focus was to make sure her daughter would get better, but she also wanted me to not feel insecure. She is an incredible warrior and I witnessed her strength firsthand throughout my journey.

After they had talked privately, she was brought to my room. As the doctor spoke to me, my mom remained silent. She knew if she acted afraid, I would feel afraid. Children look to their parents to show them how to feel in unknown situations. But the moment the doctor went through the list of things I would experience with chemo, specifically the mention of losing my hair, my mom and I both broke. Tears streamed down my face. I barely understood what was currently happening inside my body. What even was cancer? But losing my hair was something I very much understood. I was a young teenage girl, already not hitting it off with boys, a mouthful of braces, and insecurities running amok, but I found pride in my hair. It was thick and soft, and here was this new curveball. I was going to be bald.

A STILL SMALL VOICE

I gathered myself, and we left the hospital. The car ride was silent; neither of us knew what was appropriate to say. Then my mom asked, "Are you hungry?" I told her I was craving a Slurpee. My mom was surprised at my request because it seemed so simple. I think at that moment she would have bought me a full three-course meal. But Slurpees were a rare delicacy in our family, and I couldn't think of a better thing to have on this dark day. My mom pulled into a 7-Eleven gas station, and as she walked into the building she thought to herself, *My daughter…has cancer.* Then a tender voice responded, *Yes, but she is not going to die.* That was the turning point for my mom. She knew the journey would be hard, she knew we would have to fight, but she also knew, without a shadow of doubt, that the cancer would not kill her child. God had said so.

That evening I was so exhausted that I went straight to my room and lay down. I woke up to see my brother Dan, who was attending Shenandoah University at the time. He had jumped into his car immediately after hearing the news. The men in my family are not typically emotional. It is rare to see them brought to tears. I was shocked to see tears streaming down Dan's face as he took my hand. I remember thinking, *What is happening inside my body that would provoke this from my strong and confident brother?*

As we shared the news with friends and family, prayers were lifted, and our hearts cried out for God to give us direction. My best friend, Suzanne, told me that when she found out I had cancer, she and a few of our youth group friends lay on the sanctuary floor. They tried to work out what on earth was happening to their friend. All they could associate cancer with was death. One of the boys asked Suzanne, "Do you think she is going to die?" Suzanne lay there in silence, not having an answer for him, not having an answer for herself. My family worked through the next weeks that followed feeling numb and distracted. My sister, Jessica, even got a speeding ticket while Helena and I were with her, because she was preoccupied with what I was about to face.

*All she could focus on was the fact that this was
the last week of normalcy.*

CHAPTER TWO

THE SICK GIRL

It was March 2007 when the big appointment day came. My mom, sister, and Helena were with me when we drove down to the VCU Medical Center in Richmond, about an hour away, and walked into the Pediatric Oncology Unit. I had no idea how many kids were undergoing chemotherapy. The waiting room was packed—little toddlers with caps on playing with the plethora of toys in front of them. At one point, my sister and Helena offered their seats to a family of three who were just as confused and overwhelmed as we were. My mom filled out form after form, attacking it like the strong woman she has always been. She had her questions all written down, locked and loaded, ready to get her child better.

After more than a two-hour wait, by the time I got to an exam room I was exhausted and just wanted to sleep. My body had already started to feel different. I had no energy or appetite and was in constant pain. I lay on the examining table, eyes filled with sleep, tempted to doze off. Dr. Kahn, the kind man who would be my primary oncologist, walked us through this next season. I had osteosarcoma, a bone cancer that occurred frequently in children my age due to rapid growth spurts. Fortunately, with recent research, they found that it was easily cured and had only a 1 percent chance of return after treatment.

We had two options before us: we could take the standard chemo treatment or participate in a trial that would be guided by the National Cancer Institute. My mom and I decided that we would participate in the trial so that the research could be documented. We hoped that through this, it would better the results for other children with cancer. The plan was to have three months of chemo treatments (two weeks on, two weeks off), along with a significant leg surgery to remove the affected bone and replace it with a donor bone and metal rods. Lastly, I would then undergo three to four more months of chemo treatments to wrap it all up. Dr. Kahn explained the side effects of each drug I would be given. I tuned this out; I didn't want to think about it. All the details seemed too much for a young girl to handle. My mom, however, listened with the ears of a hawk. "For example, some of the side effects can cause learning problems (the most common being memory loss), and sometimes there are cases of fertility issues."

My mom began asking questions, so many that I genuinely could not retain each one. But this last side effect caught my attention. I was barely in my teens; the thought of children wasn't even on my mind. But would that possibility be taken away, before I even fell in love, because of something so out of my control? This was a difficult time for me. I had to weigh the risks and side effects against the dangers of cancer. How was I going to make it through seven months of this kind of pressure? My mom could see the weight of everything hanging on my shoulders. When the doctor left, she hugged me and said, "We don't have the answers, but we can lean heavily on the One who does."

At the end of our six-hour day, we were informed that I needed to use crutches. Although they had caught the cancer in the first stages, my bone was going to become weaker and weaker, and we did not want the bone to break. I had never broken a bone in my life. I was always such a careful kid, and even in dance I was very cautious—almost too cautious, placing limitations on myself and my craft. And here was this thing called cancer, threatening to break my femur bone by just walking on it. My life was all changing so quickly. *Hadn't it only been a month ago that I was performing in* The Nutcracker? *Was it not a mere four weeks ago that I was leaping across the stage, holding for applause?* I fell asleep on the ride home, as the day slowly blurred. Helena stayed the night, and we went about our sleepover as if neither of us were battling a life-changing disease. Just two friends afraid of nothing.

CHEMO BEGINS

In the first order of business, I had to have a port implanted in my chest then a week later begin chemotherapy. We had no idea what to expect. You can only feel so prepared for something like this. My mom packed us a bag of clothes and her toiletries, but as for me, Dr. Kahn said that the hospital would provide most of my necessary personal items. Upon arrival, they weighed me. I had already lost six pounds and treatment hadn't even started. We were then taken to a room to access my port before heading over to the hospital room where I would be staying for the next two weeks. The nurse took all the necessary precautions to numb the area around my port, but the moment she poked me with the needle, my reflex was to kick her. I got her pretty good and she rubbed her knee. I immediately apologized, and she reassured me I wasn't the first to react in such a way. We all had a good laugh, but it was short lived, as she proceeded to stick me with the needle again, and with full gusto.

Once we got to our room, we tried our best to see the good in our situation. There was a pull-out bed for my mom to sleep on, and they showed us the fridge filled with an abundance of Popsicles. The chemo was going to start attacking my cells (even the healthy ones), and they had found that patients with braces had issues with mouth sores, so Popsicles were going to be an absolute must. I then got to order off a lengthy menu of hospital meals (this was very exciting for me!), and I went with a hot dog. I snuggled up in my bed and turned on the TV. It kind of felt like I was on a vacation. My siblings would usually be the ones in control of the TV, but I had this entire room to myself. Then the vacation bubble burst. A nurse came in with the bag of chemo and hooked it up to my port. I was still adjusting to the lump on my chest, and it was incredibly sensitive, but the nurse tried her best to not aggravate the area too much. We sat and let the chemo work its way into me. Suddenly and without any notice, everything came back up. That hot dog was toast. My body revolted, and it felt like the vomiting lasted for hours. It completely cleared out my stomach. I was officially exhausted emotionally, mentally, and physically. This was only the first treatment. *What was my life going to look like these next seven months?*

When the first two weeks of chemo were finally over, we packed our things, now knowing the extra items we would need to bring on our next visit—such as pajamas that buttoned down providing easier access to my port. My body felt like it had been hit by a train. All I wanted to do was sleep. I climbed into our car, an old 1991 convertible with a ripped top and flimsy build, and slept on the drive home to Fredericksburg.

Upon our arrival, everyone was excited to see my mom and me. For the past two weeks, they had been living off of ramen and mac and cheese. I felt hungry for the first time in a long time and enjoyed some bread rolls my mom had picked up on our way home. In my last weigh-in I had dropped another six pounds. So, carbs were welcomed by both my family and doctors. I plopped down onto the bean bag chair my brother had brought for me, and I zoned out. There was so much life and chatter in my house, but I felt dead. I felt non-existent in that moment. Empty. After a while of staring off into the distance in a thoughtless daze, I got up and went to take a warm bath.

We were home for two nights when the first fever hit. We had been warned that if I got a fever, it could mean that I had an infection, possibly in my port. My mom ran a bath of lukewarm water, in hopes that it would cool me down, and helped me get into the tub. She needed to assess the next moves and sincerely hoped that we could get the fever down and not have to run back to VCU. We had just gotten home, and she had barely had time to spend with the other kids and her husband. The house was a mess and in dire need of some TLC. She hadn't even had a chance to unpack our hospital bag. But the fever did not subside, and she quickly grabbed what she needed, and we were off to Richmond again. This would become a constant in our lives—we slept more at the hospital than in our own beds, and we never did get the full two weeks home.

In order for us to go home after each treatment, the doctors would test the level of chemo still in my bloodstream. While the treatment should take only a few days to run its course, more often than not it would take around ten days, or I would have a fever. Either one prevented us from going home, and I felt like defeat was a constant companion in my life. I had been a part of planning a Sweet Sixteen surprise party for Suzanne and was supposed to be going home to attend the party that weekend, but my counts were not good. We waited until absolutely the last minute in hopes that I would be able to go. Eventually, I had to make the heartbreaking call to Helena that I would not be a part of kidnapping Suzanne and surprising her at the Cheesecake Factory.

As weeks turned into months, I began to believe the lies that my friends did not miss me. I saw posts on Facebook of parties and events, with no invitations extended. When I would get to go home and attend church with my family, my friends often wouldn't know what to say, and many attempts at conversation would be met with awkward silence. As an adult, I now look back and understand—we were all just kids. Suzanne later opened up and said that she had a hard time communicating with me because she didn't want me to feel sad about missing out on life. They were trying their hardest to support their sick friend, not wanting to say or do the wrong thing.

THE LAST THREE STRANDS

As I grew weaker with treatment, my ability to attend church and other events became utterly impossible. I also began to lose my hair. It had been holding up for about three months, which amazed the nurses and doctors, who often see far quicker hair loss. I would avoid brushing it as much as possible, but lying in bed all day would cause serious knots and rat's nests. We prayed that God would allow me to keep my hair. I had heard that there were a few patients who never lost it, and I had hope that I would be one of them. But sadly, strands would fall. God was merciful and allowed me to keep my hair for three months of chemo treatment. My hair would fall out from the bottom up, so it just proceeded to appear shorter in length. Then one day, my mom noticed the first bald spot. She braided my hair to cover it, and that worked for a while. One night in our hospital room, she told me that she needed to brush my hair. She tenderly warned me that other bald spots might be revealed. I wept with each stroke of the brush. My mom eventually had to close our room door, as the sobs were so loud. The next couple of weeks proved rough on my hair, and other than a few stragglers, it all fell out.

One day while I was home, my mom was helping me to get dressed for the day. My body had become so frail and fragile that I did not have the energy to dress myself. I had dropped a total of 40 pounds, and at just 105 pounds, bones were rearing their ugly head. My sister walked in as my mom was helping me. She stopped for a moment and then whispered something in my mom's ear, to which my mom proclaimed, "Jessica Marie! Don't say that!" Of course, I wanted to know what was said. After some pleading, Jessica confessed, "I don't mean to say this rudely...but you kind of look like Gollum."

Lord of the Rings is still one of my favorite movies, but to be compared to Gollum, I was not so pleased. However, as I leaned over and looked in the mirror, I burst out laughing. I did look like Gollum! I was skin and bones, gaunt-looking with long legs and arms, and here I was, bald headed with the three strands of hair that were holding on for dear life. We all laughed and started speaking to each other in Gollum's voice. That is my family for you—finding laughter in dark tunnels.

In order to eradicate my Gollum persona, my mom was putting in some serious wig research. We *needed* to find a wig. But the ones I saw in catalogs didn't look right to me. There were no lace-front wigs like you see on Instagram nowadays, and even if there were, my family didn't have the money to buy one. I was also afraid at the thought of my wig falling off or getting stuck on something. What if a mean boy wanted to pull a prank and rip off my wig for a big reveal? I was so sad about losing my hair, and a wig felt like just another tragic display of my situation. My mom was in close contact with the social worker at the hospital, who had given her a list of companies that helped kids with cancer get free or inexpensive wigs.

As my mom was looking at the list, the very last one on the page caught her eye: Hair Club for Kids. When she spoke to them on the phone, they explained that it was not a wig but a hair system. They made the piece with real hair, fitted it to the client's head measurements, glued it directly onto the scalp with medical-grade adhesive, and cut and styled it once it was in place. You could even have it dyed with highlights or a fun color. This company had originally specialized in hair pieces for men and women who were experiencing hair thinning, but they expanded to helping cancer patients. They provided children undergoing chemo with three hair systems per year until their treatments ended or they turned eighteen.

This process made patients feel more like themselves, because not only was the hair being cut right on their head, in whatever style they desired, but they could shower and sleep with it on.

My mom told the social worker the company we chose. She was surprised, as she'd never even heard of this company before and had no idea it was on the paperwork she had given my mom. We felt it was a legitimate "God moment"—He had truly slipped it onto the page. The social worker was ecstatic about being able to spread this news to other families. My hair systems were all beautiful and glued securely. I felt confident for the first time in a long time.

SICK AND TIRED

The months that I was undergoing chemotherapy, I wasn't sick just while I was having treatment, I was sick all the time. My car sickness (which was already very much a thing) became especially heightened. One evening, Jessica had taken me out with my friends Suzanne and Sarah. We were on our way back to the house when I asked if she would be okay with stopping to get us all the sacred Slurpee. She agreed, and we were thrilled. But as we were five minutes from my house, a rush of nausea came over me. I cried out that I was going to throw up and needed a bag. To my sister's dismay, there was no bag present, then the craziest thing happened—Sarah blurted, "Here, just throw up in my hands." So, what did I do? I actually did it! I cannot believe I threw up in someone's hands! That is a good friend right there (though with her small hands it still ended up all over Jessica's car).

Frankly, I don't think anyone likes to read about someone uncontrollably vomiting, but this had a huge importance to me at age fifteen. I had felt all alone in the hospital and questioned my worth, so when I was with friends and would get sick, it really showed me that I was valued and loved. For my brother's bar mitzvah, for instance, I was fresh into chemo life, had lost all of my hair, and was waiting for the appointment with Hair Club for Kids. I was wearing a cheaper wig we had bought specifically for this event. Simply attending the morning service was exhausting, so during the three-hour break following the service, Suzanne had invited me over to her house to get dressed in our formal wear and have some down time before the evening reception. I remember arriving at her house and immediately asking if I could lie down. I slept for a good thirty minutes and awoke to a sudden nausea that I couldn't contain. I rushed to the bathroom and, before I could even call out for Suzanne, she was there. She held my wig away from my face (which honestly, we could have just taken off at that point!) and rubbed my back. When I was finished, she took me back to bed and went to clean the bathroom. Moral of the story: find yourself friends who have your back even in the messy, and I mean messy, moments. They are lifelong.

Treatments continued. Instead of dance recitals and sleep-overs, my day to day consisted of doctors and chemotherapy. My nurses, doctors, and residents were all fantastic. I became fast friends with them, and they brought so much joy into my day. One of the nurses, Whitney, told me that the other nurses would fight over who would get me for the day or night shift. That blessed my heart. However, there was one day that I was not the perfect patient. I had recently gotten my braces removed because the mouth sores were so severe, and I was incredibly inconsistent with wearing my retainers. One day, I felt motivated to wear them and I was determined to do better. A nurse I hadn't seen before came in and told me I needed to take a medicine orally. However, my mom had just talked to the doctor, and he had said I was no longer required to take that medicine. We told the nurse this information, to which she replied that her instructions still informed her of my need to take it morning and night. I refused, and she persisted. I was not going to take my retainers out in order to take the thick and foul-tasting medication. Eventually, though, she won. I angrily removed my retainers and threw them at the end of my bed, where she was standing, and swallowed the medicine.

When she left, my mom immediately reprimanded me. I did feel pretty guilty about my actions. The next morning, I wrote the nurse an apology letter explaining that I hadn't been very good at wearing my retainers, which was my fault, and I shouldn't have taken it out on her. We were able to mend our relationship, and when Christmas rolled around, she was on my gift list. I cannot express enough the fantastic nurses I was blessed to know and the memories I will forever have.

THE HELP OF FRIENDS

After my first major surgery, where they replaced six inches of bone, my ability to get around was incredibly limited. I had a large brace that prohibited my knee from any movement. On top of that, I was being pumped with fluids because I wasn't able to hydrate enough on my own. It was the ideal equation for a perfect storm. My mom—who had become much like a dorm mom, befriending all the parents—had overheard a new family seeking help and went to their aid while I was asleep. I woke up with an insane urge to pee. I couldn't walk by myself, let alone ring my bell quick enough. My bladder released, and I felt like a four-year-old who had just wet the bed. My night nurse, Shiloh, rushed in and, without me even having to say what happened, she swooped me up and helped me into the bath. I couldn't look at her, I was so ashamed. As soon as she remade the bed, she came and got me. As she helped me to sit down, she said, "Man, if I was as pumped with fluids as you are, I would be wetting the bed every fifteen minutes." We both laughed, and she said to call her if I needed anything else.

I also had a resident who took a lot of interest in me as his patient. He would tell me funny stories of his experience working at Pizza Hut and how he and his friend were the original "cheese in the crust" creators. My other residents, though significant, were unable to stay around and chat. So, I appreciated his efforts to make me smile. He noticed one day that I was reading Robert Jordan's *The Wheel of Time*, and the next time I saw him, he brought me three more books in the series. That was such a big gesture. I was just a kid trying to get through treatment after treatment, but I felt seen. I felt like these people were not merely my doctors and nurses but my friends.

They weren't the only people who came through for me. Friends and family helped with rides when our vehicle was unreliable; they sent food home to my family and were quick to send help when needed. As treatments went on, my cravings got weird and intense. I had no appetite and could never keep anything down, but in the rare moments of hunger, I craved greasy food. I wanted specific things, though: onion rings, Olive Garden breadsticks, Taco Bell, or Pizza Hut with stuffed crust. And let us not forget the sacred Slurpee that friends brought as an offering when they would visit. Because there was nothing I craved near the hospital, my mom would reach out to the masses, and the number of people who came through was incredible. One time, a crazy craving hit for Pizza Hut stuffed crust. I had a roommate who had never tried it before, so I told her all the delicious details about it. As it was nine in the morning, not too many people were available to bring this by. My mom's best friend, Ann, asked her son to answer the call and at nine that night, after a long workday, he drove to the hospital with a stuffed crust pizza. My roommate was a foster child who was in the hospital for abuse and was the smallest eight-year-old I had ever seen. I was very excited to share with her the delight of the stuffed crust pizza. She hopped on over to my bed and sat with me, eating pizza to our heart's content, while we watched a movie forgetting how grim our life currently was.

Regardless of how good it tasted, however, the food never stayed down, and my body had lost every ounce of fat. The sick thing was, I was secretly pleased with my weight loss, as I had struggled with my self-image for a long time. I had always been athletic, so I was often bigger than other girls my age. I envied the girls who wore tiny clothing from the popular, trendy brands, knowing that not only would I never fit into that clothing, I also could not afford them. My mind had been beaten down by the devil with lies that I was not thin enough, I was not pretty enough, I was never going to be *enough*. When my body started losing weight, I saw an out. I saw myself finally being able to fit into my friends' clothing and feeling more normal beside them. I didn't notice until later in my life how thin I had become. Fragile. I was so small that my head no longer fit my body. One day in our youth group, we found a child-size medium jacket in the lost and found. One of the boys I was crushing on told me to try it on, and to my amazement, it fit. We all laughed, and I wore it around the rest of the night. I felt like I had accomplished a milestone. This would lead to years of toxic thoughts and eating disorders, which I'll cover more in-depth later on.

A PIT OR A POTHOLE?

We were nearing the last two months of chemotherapy, my leg was healing nicely, and I was starting to walk on my own. But, when we went in for a check-up, I did not feel right. I was typically exhausted and fatigued, but something felt different. I had slept during the car ride and was feeling groggy, so my mom offered to wheel me into the oncology office. It was like my hearing just went away. I could not hold my head up; I was unaware of people speaking to me. I did not realize my body was shutting down. As soon as they rolled me in to see Dr. Kahn, after a quick assessment, he realized something was wrong. It turned out that my white blood count was drastically low and my heart was being affected. They immediately gave me a blood transfusion, and I fell asleep.

I remember so little from that day. I recall, though, waking up in the PICU (pediatric ICU) and finding out that one of the chemotherapy drugs was severely affecting my heart. If they did not stop that specific chemo immediately, it could be detrimental. They informed me that because I was already greatly affected, I would need to be on digoxin (a heart medication) most likely for the rest of my life. When the doctors left, and it was just my mom and me, we cried together. It felt like it was one thing after another, storm after storm. One of the things that was supposed to heal me had hurt me in a huge way. But my God is sovereign, and He is persistent in His goodness. After six months of being on digoxin, miraculously my heart was completely restored, and I no longer needed to take it. What had felt like a deep, dark pit in the road turned out to be only a pothole. God had told my mom all those months before that I would not die, and He is not a God who lies.

After my days in the PICU, my prognosis was turning out good! We had two more chemo sessions and then *freedom*. My mom had continuously used the phrase "the light at the end of the tunnel" throughout the seven months, and I could finally see it. My leg was heading toward recovery, and I was walking like a champ. I began to dream again! My family began to dream again. We had fought cancer and won! We still had countless doctor's appointments, check-ins, and physical therapy that would be our lives for a long while, but we got through the messy part. I could see it.

It was right in front of me—the light
at the end of the tunnel.

CHAPTER THREE

A GLIMMER OF HOPE

After my last week of chemo was complete, I was on cloud nine. I experienced sheer joy, knowing that my hair would begin to grow again, and I'd be back home with my family and seeing my friends regularly. All of this had me ecstatic. I did still have frequently scheduled doctor appointments to continue bone scans and checkups, but there was hope. Hope that this was all going to be just part of my past very, very soon.

At one of the first appointments post chemotherapy, the nurse gave my mom and me a rundown of what my life was going to look like for the next couple of years. She told us that for the next year we would be doing a bone scan every three months. Over time, the scans would become less frequent. She let us know that they would be watching me for the next five years to make sure the cancer did not return. In most cases they found that if patients made it past the five-year mark, they were deemed completely cancer free and could breathe a sigh of relief.

The nurse reminded me that osteosarcoma is one of the easiest cancers to cure, with only a 1 percent chance of it ever returning. I was told that ten years prior they were doing chemotherapy on osteosarcoma children and amputating the infected limb, only to find that the cancer would spread to their lungs. For these reasons, they had started doing chemo before and after the surgery. She was very pleased with the fact that amputation was a very slim prospect at this point in their research. However, she needed to make me aware that if the cancer did come back, they would potentially need to amputate my leg. As the words flowed from her mouth, I barked back at her, "I'm a dancer. If they amputate my leg, then you might as well just let me die because I would have no desire to live." She paused, and then went on with the appointment.

I believed those words with everything inside me. I would have no desire to live if I couldn't dance. Dance was my identity. It was what made me Melissa Eadie. I craved the stage, launching myself into the air, gracefully moving through the choreography. I loved how dance made me feel free. How I could express my emotions and leave them all out there on the dance floor. I made a little comment to God before I laid the concern to rest. I said to Him, *God, you allowed me to walk through seven months of chemo and a huge leg surgery that has taken away so much of me already. Please, God, please don't let this world also take my leg.* That was the end of that. The thought never even crossed my mind again after that appointment.

GROWING FEAR OF REJECTION

My life started to feel normal again, almost like chemo had never taken so much energy out of me. I was allowed to attend dance classes as long as I did no leaps and was mindful of myself. Dance was also accompanied by weekly physical therapy appointments to help my knee regain mobility. A few of my friends had gotten me new leotards to wear. In my new tiny body, I felt like a beautiful prima ballerina. During one of the classes, we were at the bar doing grand battements (a move in which you throw one of your legs into the air and bring it back down). I had no idea the range of my flexibility at this point and kicked myself in the head. I made eye contact with my dance instructor, and we both paused in shock of what had just happened. Then we burst out in laughter. Dancing made me forget all the doctors' appointments that were scheduled, the massive scar on my right leg, and the fact that I was still wearing a hair system. But my hair was growing back! In a month or so I knew I would feel comfortable enough to not need it.

Another exciting event was that I was given the opportunity to travel to Israel with my youth group. However, what I didn't realize was that there was a great amount of tension among the group. Someone had gifted the trip to me, so I had not experienced the fundraising process like the other kids. Because of this, some of my friends were annoyed at my free ride. I had no idea the can of worms I had opened by accepting this gift. I think back about it now and realize that they were simply kids who had worked hard to make this trip happen for themselves. Yet, here was one of their fellow friends not having to lift a finger in order to go. They had no idea what my life had looked like for the last seven months. They hadn't seen the vomit-filled, fatigued, energy-less hospital life I had just gone through. But I also hadn't seen their months and months of fundraisers, hot car-wash days, and yard raking. If only I could go back in time and tell my sixteen-year-old self that it was a simple misunderstanding on both sides. But young minds are greatly influenced, and I spent many, many years completely petrified of one thing: rejection.

I was so afraid of being rejected that I resorted to being silly, loud, and always aching to be the center of attention. I didn't know how to act around boys. Instead of acting like a calm human being, I made sure to get their attention in any way possible, which was never the right attention in the first place. I came off more annoying than lovable. I was witnessing my friends being pursued by guys, but I felt unseen and undesired. I felt like it took a long time for people to not see me as "the sick girl." I wanted to be able to get back to a normal life. I wanted to date nice boys and be told I looked pretty as I glided down a winding staircase. I wanted to forget about those agonizing months at the hospital. After so many months of feeling like death, I wanted to live again. However, I was searching in the wrong places. I was image obsessed, with an eating disorder gaining hold of me. My obsession with boys was increasing, begging for them to pay me any type of attention. My mind was consumed with the future, ready to get these last months as far from me as possible. I forgot all the things God had taught me. I was so caught up in the things I had missed out on that I lost track of the insane growth and journey God had just walked me through. What I viewed as a season of suffering and sadness, He had used for maturity and growth. He had taught me in those months how to be patient, how to not take family for granted, how to love better, and how to cherish the little things, though at the time, I couldn't see the full picture.

COMFORTING OTHERS

As time went by, I saw how God wanted to use my story. By having cancer and going through the chemotherapy process, I was able to speak to others battling cancer themselves or about to go through the process with a loved one. One of those people suffering from news of a cancer diagnosis was Suzanne's mom. When my friend called to tell me the news of her mom's diagnosis with colon cancer, she was a wreck. But, she had hope because she had walked with me through it, and was seeing me on the mend and healing. She asked me if I wouldn't mind coming over and giving her mom some advice, as they were getting ready for their first chemotherapy appointment. I was so scared, as they were truly like a second family to me. I feared that my advice would be of no help. What could I say to help ease her mind regarding one of the scariest words, *cancer*? I felt inadequate for the task, but I wanted to do whatever I could.

As we sat in their living room, the atmosphere was shockingly joyful. There were laughter and hugs, a family united, not just together but united in Christ. Once everyone was sitting down, I felt the pressure rise in me, knowing now was the time to give some spot-on advice. I blurted out, "You're going to want to pack your own toothbrush and toothpaste." Everyone laughed as I spoke with such conviction. I found this advice to be essential. I went on, telling her to pack her own pillowcase, as those at the hospital can smell like bleach—and one of the symptoms I experienced from chemo was an enhanced sense of smell. Our hospital social worker provided brand new pillowcases to us kiddos, with all sorts of fun prints (mine was green with zoo animals), and because I could wash it at home it changed the game entirely. I also told them that company was an absolute must. When my family would come to visit me in the hospital it would cheer me up for days! I remember one time my entire family came for a visit. I had an inexpensive wig lying on a mannequin head beside my bed, and before I knew it, my family proceeded to try it on. This included my dad and all my brothers. I expressed to Suzanne and her family how important it was to laugh and make good memories. My advice seemed so small…I didn't have anything really huge to offer, but I could tell it gave them peace. I left knowing that they were going to make it, that this would just be a season in their life as well.

The months flew by and life was getting back to normal. But, there was a dark habit continuing to grow inside me that I hid from the light. When I finished chemotherapy, I was 98 pounds at 5 foot 8. After a few months out of treatment, I was up to 125 pounds. I panicked. I was constantly hungry, so I knew I couldn't just stop eating. I decided that I was going to purge my food after each meal, just as I did when I was undergoing chemotherapy. It wasn't any different, right? Recalling this part of my past, it amazes me how someone can make an excuse for anything if it's what they want to do. The devil is a master manipulator, an expert at deceit. I look back at photos and cringe at my dark circles and sunken eyes, with protruding bones and frail stature. I remember lying on my back in front of my mirrored closet and seeing how close I could get my belly to the floor. I would wrap my hands around my thigh to see if I could get my thumbs to touch. I would gorge at meals and then excuse myself like I was going to go take a shower and turn the water on to hide the noise. I relished comments like, "Wow, Mel, you really are just skin and bones," or "Literally, look at your arms! They're non-existent." These were not compliments; however, little did those people know how much they were fueling me to continue the road of bulimia.

There I was, struggling through an eating disorder, fearing any kind of rejection at all, and still not processing through everything that had happened the last seven months of my life. I remember our new neighbors came over for a game night. They had two sons, and I was set on grabbing the oldest's attention. I was rail thin, still wearing my hair system, and had no eyebrows, but I decided to go for it. I sat beside him during game night and tried to have a conversation. When that didn't seem to work, I tried the "ignore him" game, which was not successful either. I know, shocking right? I had matured in so many areas, grown up so fast, been a trooper in the hospital, but I felt like I missed out on learning the vital skills of how to act appropriately around boys. I was sixteen and acting like a ten-year-old on the playground.

That evening was a hot mess. I was hunting down that poor kid, giving him no space to breathe, and he was not having it. He eventually asked his parents if he could walk home, and he left before we even got through the second game. He paid me no attention as he walked out the door. So, what did I do? I went upstairs, and I laid on my back in front of that darn mirror and watched to see how close my stomach could get to the floor. I then assessed my hair, instantly jumping to the assumption that he judged me for having been through chemo. I felt that he saw me only as the "sick girl" next door. I would fall into this trap for many years to come, playing the "sick girl" card whenever I felt rejected. I was so quick to play the victim, but really, I was the problem.

THE ONE IN CONTROL

I decided to move on from dance to theater because I still wanted to be an actress. I joined the Christian Youth Theater (CYT) with my brother Michael and it was suddenly very easy to get past that "sick girl" role. No one there knew that season of my life, and though I wasn't afraid to talk about it, it wasn't something I dwelt on. Through this theater experience, I would meet some forever friends of mine who would go through numerous journeys with me. Auditions were always ridiculously filled with anxiety on my end, but my brother thrived. After each audition we would praise each other and then wait for the call list. I loved doing shows with my brother. We were two peas in a pod. We loved singing together and making parody videos, which I would edit and post on YouTube. We were crazy on the dance floor and just in general. He understood me. It was so fun to play off each other and watch people's reactions. We would always cheer each other on in whatever parts we were given, and I got to see my brother come alive on stage.

During my first production with CYT, I was able to put aside my eating disorder. I had tried to continue purging the first week of rehearsals, but my lack of energy made it very difficult to get through the day. A few productions later, while we were doing the show *Aladdin*, I got hit with whooping cough the weekend we opened. I had no idea of my diagnosis, so I pushed through a crazy cough that just wouldn't quit. During the show, there was a scene where I needed to run from one side of the stage around to the other side through a long back hallway. This, of course, sent me into a coughing spell. To make matters worse, the cough was so bad it would frequently cause me to throw up. I remember the actor playing Iago sat with me numerous times backstage. I would have a cough attack that would eventually lead to me heaving into a trash can, and he would act like nothing was wrong. In the weirdest, most messed up way, I was grateful for the cough. I had really started to put on weight, as my eating habits were similar to my cravings during chemo. I devoured lots of fried food and carbs but was not throwing it up, and I was feeling bloated and disgusting. I look back at photos from that time and think, *Wow, I was finally starting to look like a human being!* But at the time I would look in the mirror and think to myself, *You are so fat and ugly.*

Perhaps you have struggled with similar thoughts regarding your image, or you have an eating disorder of your own. If so, I want to address that, understanding that it's not an instant fix kind of thing. Body dysmorphia is an actual head game. I struggled with it from ages eleven to twenty-three. I know firsthand the fight that it takes to beat something you feel has become embedded in your bloodstream. I in no way want to minimalize the journey that it will take, but I want to share one major thing I did that began the process of overcoming—and that was run to the one Person who I knew saw me in the truest light. Here are just a few examples of what He has to say about us, His very own creation:

> So God created man in His own image, in the image and likeness of God He created him; male and female He created them.   (Genesis 1:27, AMP)

It's amazing that this statement is in the first chapter of the entire Bible. It was so important to God that He made it first-chapter material: you are made in the very image of our awesome God! You are significant in His eyes. Maybe you're thinking,

Okay, I hear that verse all the time; it's everyone's go-to when someone is struggling with their image or worth. Can you give me something more? I sure can:

> Does a clay pot dare argue with its maker, a pot that is like all the others? Does the clay ask the potter what he is doing? Does the pot complain that its maker has no skill?
>
> (Isaiah 45:9, GNT)

My dear reader, why do we question our God about our worth? He created you, a beautiful specimen, and He takes great pride in you. I had to learn through many years of hurting that He is the ultimate artist, the ultimate potter. I had to request that I would see myself through His eyes and not the eyes of the world. It grieves my heart how much pressure we put on ourselves to be a certain thing for this world when in the end the Bible says:

> Charm is deceptive, and beauty is fleeting; but a woman who fears the LORD is to be praised. (Proverbs 31:30, NIV)

So, there it is—the hard truth. In the grand scheme of things, our outward appearance isn't even a factor when determining our true beauty. I was skin and bones but struggling with an ugly heart. If God made us in His own image, and I find myself obsessively staring in the mirror, image consumed, telling myself how absolutely disgusting I am, how disrespectful, and honestly dumb, of me to tell Him all the mistakes He made! He made me a beautiful creation. I was caught up in the fact that I wasn't born with six-pack abs, able to prance around in size zero pants. But, friend, you need to take it from someone who has been there, done that. What we value most in this life should not be our appearance, because physical beauty is fleeting. As hard as that is to hear, it absolutely is. You may be someone who doesn't know the Jesus I know, and you're feeling like I just threw a lot of Scripture at you from a book you don't believe in. Whoever you are, you didn't pick up this book by chance. I want so badly for you to hear me: when it comes down to it all, an eating disorder will leave you more broken than when you first decided you weren't enough.

You may think you're in control if you choose to purge, but in reality the eating disorder is controlling you. Do not for one second believe the lie that you're in control. The devil preys on our insecurities. He loves that as humans we have so many! It took years for me to see how God views me and to realize how broken I had become. I was harboring anger toward friends who could eat whatever they wanted, not gaining a pound. But you know what? They were dealing with their own insecurities! We need to stop seeing other individuals as competition and start seeing them as partners, as teammates. This world is hard enough without tearing each other down to make ourselves feel somewhat more valuable. Control is a game. We win once we realize the only one who is really in control is Jesus. We must stop trying to take matters into our own hands. What a life we are missing out on. When we start to loosen our grip on our own lives and ask God to stop the back-breaking spiral of what we think we need to be, that is when doors open. That is when release happens. That is when you really start living. It is going to take time, but it can be done. I wish I could go back in time and tell myself all these things before bulimia got such a hold on me, but since I don't have a time machine, I don't want to waste another moment doubting that I am anything less than an incredible creation.

CRUTCHES AND ALL

Michael and I were now doing a production of *Alice in Wonderland*, and we had just completed the first weekend of shows, with one more weekend to go. My dear friend Sarah Bower was Alice, and I just happened to be her counterpart, Tall Alice. Michael was playing the role of Tweedledum. It was such a fun show—I especially enjoyed the dance routine in the finale. As my role was a little smaller, being only in the scene where Alice grows, I made sure to go all out when I danced. I remember my cheeks burning at the end of every show from smiling so hard. We packed everything up at the school where we performed and left for our week in between shows. Two days into our break, as I was starting to get up and ready for school, a shooting pain went through my knee and I couldn't walk. I screamed out to my mom, who ran upstairs and burst into my room. I sobbed thinking that the cancer must be back—it felt so similar. It was also incredibly swollen around the knee. Darkness washed over all the light at the end of the tunnel that I had been seeing. We immediately made an appointment with the doctor's office. He examined my knee, expressing that it felt like fluid had built up around the area. He would need to insert a needle and draw out some of the fluid to test it. To my dismay, he took a giant needle to my knee and inserted it as far as he could. Tears flooded my eyes as I was filled with disbelief and pain. It felt like yesterday that I was dealing with this kind of stuff...would it ever end?

The next day, they gave us the lab results: staph infection. Apparently, it had been lying dormant since my leg surgery and had reared its ugly head because of all my activities. They were able to put me on an antibiotic and the watching game began. I had hope that by that weekend I would be able to walk again and dance, but Friday rolled around and I was still on crutches. I walked into the school for our last weekend of shows so defeated, so sad that this was my life. I passed a very sweet girl they had called in to read for my part, and I just broke down in the hallway. The director, Marilyn Scott, told me that the understudy would be used only if I felt I couldn't go on stage. I told her that I couldn't walk and would need to use my crutches. I expressed my sorrow for the possibility of ruining the show. She looked at me and said with love and honesty, "I am not removing you from Tall Alice. If you want to go on stage, then you will go on stage, crutches and all."

The crew even created a decorated bench that had wheels (we called it "the cloud"). Sarah and the actress who played Small Alice wheeled me out on stage for the finale and I got to dance with the cast. However, it did prove to be slightly dangerous when they let go of "the cloud" as we all waved to the audience and I found myself rolling toward the edge of the stage. Staying in character, I chose not to say anything, but luckily Sarah saved me just in the nick of time. I thanked everyone for their kindness and willingness to work with me. To say it wasn't obvious that I was pretty messed up would be a lie, but we got through the weekend! I felt so much joy and love from the people around me. I couldn't have asked for better friends. At the cast party for the show, they surprised me with an arrangement of "Lean on Me," which not only made me and my family cry, but brought the entire room to tears.

The staph infection caused my leg to hurt and swell, but each time the pain subsided with the help of antibiotics. I was cleared to resume dancing, but my leg never fully regained range of motion. I was so uncomfortable, and my movements seemed forced and rigid. On top of needing to decrease my physical activity, my leg continued to grow stiffer. To add to what already seemed to be a nightmare, a wound began to form and, to spare your stomach, I will just say, staph did as staph does. I would battle this infection for a little over a year. In that year, much would happen.

BEATING THE STAPH INFECTION

I had been given a plan of action on how to beat the staph infection that was causing all kinds of havoc in my life. The plan was to remove the new bone I had been given and replace it with a bone filled with antibiotics. Then, I would have an IV attached to my arm that would pump more antibiotics into me. Though I wasn't excited about lugging around a bag of medicine, I was excited to get this mess dealt with and finally get back to a normal life.

In a freak turn of events, the East Coast was hit with an earthquake. I was sitting in my Italian class with my professor, Mrs. Anglin, and the entire wall launched out at us! I had never experienced an earthquake in my entire life. I thought that we had been hit with a bomb or that the construction crew working on the school had made a terrible mistake. We all ran outside panicked and completely confused about what had just occurred. It was a very hot day and everyone's adrenaline was pumping. No one had cell phone service, so we were all stranded, not knowing how our families were doing.

After the earthquake, classes were moved to a different building or online until the building could be repaired. I had a large class project coming up, and I was stressing big time. Then one night, the stomach pain came. Excruciating pain in my abdomen that felt so different than any I had experienced before. Something was wrong. I pushed through the week with this pain, barely able to stand up straight, and eventually I asked my professor if I could send him my PowerPoint without an oral presentation. He understood and accepted that I would not be able to give my presentation in person.

After a few more days of that awful pain, suddenly red dots arose on my skin. We realized this was pretty urgent. It turned out that I had been on the antibiotics for far too long, as we were never told to stop them. It had caused two ulcers to form in my intestines as well as a disorder called HSP (Henoch-Schonlein Purpura). My small blood vessels were inflamed causing bleeding in the skin. This disorder was also affecting my joints, intestines, and kidneys. We checked into a local hospital, which was very low staffed, and what was meant to take three days to resolve ended up taking an entire week. My surgery to fix the staph infection was right around the corner. I was so disappointed to be going from one hospital bed almost immediately to another.

I was discharged and was finally home in my own bed. But the peace and relief that washed over me would be short-lived.

CHAPTER FOUR

DON'T LOOK DOWN

The day came for the big surgery, August 31, 2011. My mom and I packed up our overnight bag, hugged our family goodbye, and headed off for the next part of our journey. I say "our" because my family is a big part of my story. God knew exactly the people I would need with me to walk through this life. I have never met a harder worker than my father, a more tender-hearted person than my mom, better defenders of me than my brothers, and a stronger (sometimes hardheaded!) person than my sister. My story is nothing without the credit I must give to them.

Once at the hospital, I changed into my gown, said goodbye to my mom, and nonchalantly was strolled into the surgery room. I remember the nurse was very chatty, and I liked that, as I was a talker and enjoyed the conversation. It eased my mind. We talked about my trip to Israel and how I got to go scuba diving with the dolphins. Soon they had me counting backward from ten, and before I knew it I was waking up in recovery. I felt like I was there for only a second, then I awoke in my hospital room. With sleep in my eyes, I looked up to see my father standing beside my bed. *What is my dad doing here? Oh wait...my entire family is here...What is happening?* Panic arose in me. I was supposed to be going home that night so there was no reason for my family to have come.

My dad tried to start a casual conversation, asking how I felt, but the silence in the room could not go unnoticed. He took my hand and said with tears welling, "The doctor is about to come in. He needs to talk to you." I had seen my father cry only one other time—when his father passed away. I asked my dad, "What does the doctor want to talk to me about?" As my dad choked back another tear, the doctor came in as if on cue. The doctor explained to me that as he was finishing the surgery and was getting ready to close me up, his hand grazed something that didn't feel right. At closer examination, he saw a tumor was hiding in a ligament behind my knee. In order to remove the tumor, he had to remove the whole ligament, therefore, my leg was no longer functioning. I attempted to wiggle my leg, eventually trying to whip it around to no avail.

A rush of emotions washed over me and threatened to drown me in the repeated waves. When I was a child I had an awful experience at the beach where no matter what I did, a wave would crash upon me before I could stand to flee from it. I would hit the bottom of the ocean, come up to gasp for air, and immediately be pushed down again. It was as if I were reliving that moment. I begged him to explain to me what all of this meant. Would I need to endure more chemotherapy? Would I need to have another surgery? He said that the only option they had was to amputate or run the risk of the cancer returning and migrating to my lungs. Tears exploded; I was done for. The room spun and people's faces blurred. I had no idea who was standing where. I told the doctor, "No, no honey, no…no," which was something my brother Michael and I would say back and forth to each other when being extra silly. My body was trying to grasp for anything normal or funny at this moment, anything that could potentially make this all a joke. This had to be the cruelest joke ever…*Please, God,* I wept. My body exhausted and attempting to escape the grogginess of the anesthesia, eyelids growing heavy, I fought to not accept defeat, but then the faces around me faded to black. With that, I fell into a restless sleep.

THE ONE PERCENT

When I awoke again, my parents had discussed the next steps with the doctor. They needed to do the surgery pretty urgently, the next day to be exact. My dad begged them to push it out just one day, because the next day was my sister's birthday, and he didn't want the day to be tainted. However, they couldn't budge.

On and off that day I would suddenly fall asleep, like my body was shutting down from the sorrow I was feeling inside. I can't lie and say I didn't think about what I told the nurse when she warned me that this could be a possibility…She had said there was only a 1 percent chance it could ever return. How was I special enough to be the 1 percent? You had to be kidding me! Throughout that day we had many family members and our rabbi visit, but it was truly all a blur. Six months earlier I had started a relationship with my friend Matt, and when he visited me, I found myself completely burdened with the thought, *How could he possibly want to continue down this path with me?* My heart was broken. I did not understand. Was God my friend? How could He do this to me? I was a dancer! I wanted to be an actress! Why was He taking everything away? I truly could not picture a life without my leg...How could I?

It felt like the day dragged on, like it would never come to an end. I didn't want it to end. I wanted the day to last forever so I would never face the next morning. Even with the hurt and sorrow pounding in my head, I urged God, *Please, don't let me lose everything that I have worked so hard to gain! Please don't leave me stranded! Abba, if You could, please turn this situation around and make my leg completely healed!* I was crying out and my heart felt so completely heavy. The doctors had told me that if I made it five years cancer free, then it was almost certain the cancer would not return. I was at four years and six months and here I was, so close...and yet so far. How could this be happening? The light was fading, both in my heart and in the day. I fought sleep, knowing the next time I woke up it would be to prepare for surgery and a new life.

After much tossing and turning, I slid away into sleep. I woke up in the middle of the night with a tear-soaked pillow—I couldn't get away from this nightmare even in my dreams. I turned over to find that I was not the only one awake. My dad sat in the chair beside my bed, hand on his forehead, gazing off into the distance. He acknowledged that I was awake, but for a few moments we just stared up at the hospital ceiling in complete silence. Then my dad looked at me and said in an eccentric accent, "You know, this could turn out to be a great story. Just listen to this. We come up with a great shark bite story. The biggest great white in history comes out of nowhere and *'Ahhh!'* It bit your leg clean off! You then swam back to shore, drove yourself to the hospital, and performed your own surgery." I couldn't help but smile, just a little. This was just as hard for my dad as it was for me. I was his little dancer, his baby girl. I always thought that the child undergoing the harsh circumstance suffered the most, but I realized it's actually the parents who endure the most suffering. They have to watch as their child deals with great loss and pain, while not having an ounce of control or power to help them. My heart grieves for the parents. But, alas, here was my dad attempting his best to be strong for me. After all the dad jokes and humor I've experienced in our house, here he was trying to make me laugh in a hard predicament.

He tried to encourage me the best way he knew how. But once the room fell quiet again, he became very serious. All jokes aside he said to me, "Melissa, you have two options here. You can allow this either to break you or to make you. God can still use this. You have to accept this in order to live. If you don't accept it, you'll never live again. Don't let this moment take away from everything God has done. Don't allow this to steal your joy and keep you from living a full life." Tears flooded both of our eyes as I told him I was going to try. In that very moment I felt a shift; I felt something awaken inside me. *Could it really be...peace? Could it truly be peace that despite whatever God allowed, He was still sovereign and good?* My mindset was changing. My heart was broken and dreams burned down to a crisp, but something was rising within me. I knew this was not the end of a good life. I knew that He had a plan and a purpose for me. And if it included losing my leg, I was going to let Him use me. I love this verse and would reflect on it often in the years to come:

> "The Spirit of the Sovereign Lord is on me, because the
> Lord has anointed me to proclaim good news to the poor.
> He has sent me to bind up the brokenhearted, to proclaim
> freedom for the captives and release from darkness for the

prisoners, to proclaim the year of the LORD's favor and the day of vengeance of our God, to comfort all who mourn, and provide for those who grieve in Zion—to bestow on them a crown of beauty instead of ashes, the oil of joy instead of mourning, and a garment of praise instead of a spirit of despair. They will be called oaks of righteousness, a planting of the LORD for the display of his splendor."

(Isaiah 61:1–3, NIV)

The next day came as if seconds had passed from when I shut my eyes and fell asleep. It was time to say goodbye. My family and I prayed for miraculous healing, that the ligament would reappear and that the amputation would be avoided. My dad, believing in a miracle-working God, asked the lead surgeon to please take a look at the ligament before proceeding with the amputation. He agreed to do so. As a family, we stood with faith for a complete healing, but we also trusted God's perfect will. They were quick to get me prepped for surgery that morning, but every nurse and doctor was gentle and sweet, and they didn't rush the journey to the surgery room. I felt like they were part of my family, grieving with us. As I counted backward from ten, tears streamed down my face. My mind went blank, and I went numb.

I awoke, groggy and initially confused...and then reality set in.

Don't look down, Melissa. Don't look down.

Don't. Look. Down. This was what I muttered to myself when I first awoke from my surgery. *Mel, if you look down, it's over. You're proving to yourself that this isn't just a dream. Please don't look down.* I thought that I was giving myself the perfect advice; however, I was only feeding my fears and anxieties. This was real. Eventually

I would need to come to terms with it and I would need to look down. But that moment wasn't going to be right then.

I was taken to my room where my family was waiting. Silence. Complete silence. There were no words for what had just happened. There were no words for this great loss. Slowly, immediate and extended family came in and out. My eyes red and puffy, with so little to say, I found comfort in numbers. Seeing the consistent flow of faces coming into the room throughout the day gave ease to my mind. I was hurting and barely hanging on, but my family made me feel like I had just enough strength to get through the day, and maybe that would trickle into the next day. A close family friend (more accurately, "my sister from another mister"), Christine was experiencing her own tragic loss, yet she sent a brand new iPad with my brother, Dan, making sure I knew that I was on her mind. This impacted me greatly. Despite going through an incredible life change herself, she was thinking of me. Her thoughtful act encouraged me to try to be as selfless as possible, to remember that I wasn't the only one going through a difficult time, and that I could bless others even in my pain.

LIFE WITH "FAT LOUIE"

The next day, a physical therapist (PT) was sent in to start getting me up and out of bed. The PT asked me if I thought I could work with her a little, and I said with a smile that I thought I could, but that I did not want to see my leg in the process. She understood. She did something with me lying down, with a sheet covering my leg, and then asked if I could sit on the edge of the bed. As she was helping me to sit up, I couldn't help but look down and see my leg. I immediately felt a wave of emotion rush over me, and I was undone. Tears streamed down my face uncontrollably and she knew that we were done for the day. As my mom walked the PT out of the room, I looked to my dad and said, "I know you want me to be strong. I know you want me to not allow this to break me…to lose sight of the bigger picture. But, Dad, I thought God said He would never give us more than we can handle. This totally feels like more than I can even bear!"

My dad pondered for a moment and then said, "Whatever the Lord allows to happen, it is because the Lord knows you can handle it. Because He is with you and you don't have to bear the weight alone." He said he understood that I was hurting and needed time, but that I was going to be okay. He said even if it took six months, a year, or however long it would take for me to adjust to this, the family would be there. He said, "It's up to you to determine the time you need to heal." It wouldn't be that day that I fully believed those words. It wouldn't even be the next couple of years. But if there is one thing I know with absolutely no doubt, it is that even in my pain and sorrow, God was orchestrating my comeback story. I see that now.

As my dad and I were talking, my mom met a friend of mine from CYT, Jared Elton, in the hallway. He would be the first visitor since my surgery who wasn't family. She told him that PT hadn't gone well and that I needed a moment. When I had recomposed myself and was ready for him to come in, the conversation went like this:

"Hi."

"Hi."

Awkward silence.

Proceeding to get the elephant in the room out of the way, I pointed to my leg. "Well, it's gone."

"Yes, it is," Jared replied, a little teary eyed.

"So, how ya been?"

The conversation then went on to mutual friends, what he was up to, funny hospital stories. My mom recalls how quickly the awkwardness left the room. We just jumped back into being regular teenagers talking about teenage life.

That day, several friends started to visit. By that I mean every single person I have ever known in my life. We were blessed to have been given one of the biggest rooms in the hospital. We would sometimes have ten people (not including my family) inside the room. People had to wait in the hallway because they couldn't all fit. The nurses would stop in to tell us how much fun it was listening to the laughter, singing, and words of encouragement coming from the room. I started to feel more like myself. I realized people didn't see me as a broken person; they didn't see me differently at all. We were able to go about our normal conversations and could laugh as usual. It felt so normal.

At one point throughout the busy day with people shuffling in and out, my mom came over to sit at the foot of my bed. Without thinking, she sat down—exactly where my right leg would have been. We made eye contact. I gasped, not knowing how to react, so my mom jumped up and said, "Too soon?" Then we burst out laughing. There were many moments like this. Because of the pain medication I was on, I didn't experience much phantom limb pain. However, there would be certain times that my invisible leg would start itching up a storm. The first time it happened, I screamed because I couldn't scratch it! My dad jokingly said, "Why don't you try scratching your other leg?" I took the advice, and low and behold—it actually helped!

So throughout visits I would get "random itchy invisible leg syndrome" and aggressively go at my other leg to relieve the itch.

We would burst out laughing every time. It was so outrageous. The first time I ever raised my stump to move it and see what it felt like, I did a little dance with it which brought us all to tears laughing. This was what I needed. To feel like my normal self, to be silly, to not let this change me. Speaking of stump, I absolutely hated calling it that, so I asked my nurses and family to start calling it "Fat Louie," and to this day I refer to it this way.

The days were long with visitors while physical therapy continued. The first day I stood up, the rush of blood in "Fat Louie" was excruciatingly painful. But with practice, each time I stood it got better. Therapy eventually would entail me climbing up and down stairs on crutches, building endurance, and getting around tough mazes. I was getting stronger and felt like a pro. I felt joy. I was alive, the cancer was taken care of, and no one seemed to think of me any differently than before. A couple days in, my friend Sarah Bower brought her guitar and we had a worship night in the hospital. We praised God for His goodness. While singing, I began thinking back to when I first found out I had cancer. I came home from the biopsy and asked my dad, "Why, Dad? Why do bad things happen to good people? Aren't I a good kid?" He replied, "Well, in hard times, God can use you to be a blessing to those around you."

I thought back to my days of chemo, in which I was able to speak about Jesus with my many roommates. I was able to be a display of God's love by brightening the doctors' and nurses' day by simply being kind. I was by no means perfect; just ask the nurse I basically threw my retainers at! But I do know that God loves to create beauty from ashes. My dad was right—yes, sometimes bad things do happen to good people, innocent people like children, but it's not about us. It is about the lives we have the opportunity to impact. I didn't understand what God was doing or why I lost my leg. However, I did know that He had used my circumstances before, and I wanted to be used again.

THE JOURNEY HOME

Matt would drive to the hospital every day after work to be with me. We would watch movies with my sister, which I had to be reminded that we watched because I was so doped up on morphine. I would apparently converse during the movies though I have absolutely no recollection of any of it. I was still in my college classes, but they were online at this point due to the freak earthquake. My teachers were completely understanding of the situation, but I still wanted to stay up to date as much as possible. I was taking a Shakespeare class and we had a reading assignment. Jessica offered to read for me because my pain medications made my vision weird and unfocused. She began reading, and I thought I was fully aware. Suddenly, I awoke to lights off, Matt in the corner looking exhausted and Jessica squeezed into the small hospital bed beside me. The last thing I remembered was her reading, so it kind of threw me into a panic to have such different scenery. Matt got up and walked over to laugh with me about my looniness. Then as he left to head home, I listened to Jessica soundly sleeping beside me, just as we had done as kids, and I fell into the most peaceful sleep I had had since coming to the hospital.

I was told that I would be able to stay in the hospital as long as my family and I felt we needed to, but it was coming up on day seven and I felt ready to take the journey home. I was feeling great, optimistic even. I was really just ready to get the ball rolling on the rest of my life. I even discussed the possibility of returning to classes that coming week. My parents reminded me to take it one step at a time, but I was really overflowing with optimism. The night before I left the hospital, Matt and my friend Drew decorated my crutches with peacock-feather duct tape and ribbons. They said they wanted my crutches to match my personality. I loved peacocks and would often wear peacock feathers in my hair. I was overwhelmed with love and gratitude as my friends and family had really shown up for me. They went above and beyond and were a huge reason why I was able to pick up the pieces and put myself back together, with peacock-feather duct tape.

I was recently talking to Jessica about that week in the hospital, asking for any details she remembered as I was pretty drugged for most of it. She said that she was just truly amazed at how positive I remained, and how I was joking around and laughing. I do remember laughing, and truly feeling joy. Not just happiness, but pure joy. Something clicked mentally after my dad spoke to me the night before the amputation. I knew there would be hard days, but I didn't feel broken. I didn't feel the need to focus on my loss, but to focus on what God was allowing me to gain. By the grace of God, it wasn't even an option to dwell on the negative points. Friends would rave in the hospital about how positive I was being and how strong I was. Although this made me feel good, I knew I couldn't take the credit. It wasn't my doing at all, it was all God. You can choose not to believe that, but I know who I was and how I would have handled the situation. The Melissa I knew believed it was worth dying rather than losing her leg. So I want to make it clear: God can and will supernaturally touch your life even in the darkest of times. He has the power to change your mindset; you just have to let Him.

Day seven came, and I was discharged. With IVs removed and hospital gown replaced with pajamas, now with the right pant leg tied up in a knot, I was excited to be going home. My mom wheeled me out to the car. We decided the easiest way to get in would be to slide into the back seat and place the crutches on the floor. I was ready to be home, to sleep in my own bed, and to hang out with my family (though they had visited frequently that week). The car ride was pretty quiet as my mom and I were processing through everything and were both pretty unsure of how it was all going to look in the next hour upon arrival. We stopped for our traditional Slurpee, though at this point it was primarily therapeutic.

The journey home started the next season of my life: living as an amputee.

CHAPTER FIVE

A NEW BEGINNING

As we drove up to our house and into the driveway, I began thinking about all the obstacles ahead of me. To start with, getting into the house requires walking up an incline. Then there are two options: either going up a flight of stairs to enter the side door or walking up three stairs to the front door. Once inside the house, there are several baby gates because of our dogs: two shih tzu puppies, Bella and Bandit, and my sister's cockapoo, Roscoe. More obstacles. Every day, I would have to face the seventeen stairs up and down from my bedroom. I had practiced maneuvering at the hospital, but when we practiced stairs it was only three. At home it felt like a mountain was in front of me. All of this was running through my head before we even parked. My dad came out and carried me in. Even though I had been in the hospital for only a week, my body was incredibly fatigued. He asked me where I wanted him to take me and I requested my bedroom. I felt so tired and emotionally spent, I just wanted to lie down.

Not knowing what the first night home would entail, I asked my mom to sleep with me—and I'm so glad she did. Around 1 a.m. I awoke to severe aching and a sharp pain in "Fat Louie." We had been well informed about phantom limb pain, caused by nerve endings shooting off signals to toes that were no longer there. I was given medication, and the doctors warned me that the pain could be pretty aggressive until the medicine kicked in or the nerve endings died. Even with all the preparation they tried to give me, I had no idea it would be as bad as it was. I had been on morphine in the hospital, so it had completely numbed me to any pain (other than the occasional itchiness).

The pain I experienced that night felt like being pricked by thousands of needles, then randomly bitten by a sharp-fanged animal. I began sobbing because I couldn't stop the pain and I couldn't walk it off; it just was what it was. My mom tried to console me, but I was angry at this point. I was grumpy because I was tired, but I was also upset that I truly had no control over what was happening. No amount of tears stopped the consistent pain raging through my phantom limb. On top of that, I was disappointed in myself because I was lashing out at my mom who was just trying to help me. It is pretty crazy how we can lose all awareness of how we treat people when we hurt. There's no excuse for it, but it's very easy to simply accept our bad behavior and excuse it.

The next day, one of my close friends, Cori, asked if I wanted to meet her and another friend from our theater group at the mall. My mom was prepared to help me have a restful week adjusting to being home, yet here I was ready to get out of the house and see my friends. I was so excited to attempt to go back out into civilization. I had absolutely no desire to be wheeled around in a chair and told my mom once we got to the mall that I was going to use my crutches to get to the Starbucks inside. It seemed like it took me ages. With my body still recovering from lying in a hospital bed, I was shocked at how exhausted I felt after only a few paces. I noticed a few people here and there staring at me, but for the most part, it didn't bother me. A security guard asked if we needed a wheelchair, which I politely declined. I was so focused on pushing myself to make it because I *needed* to prove to myself I could do it. I think my adrenaline was rushing out of excitement to see my friends. We finally reached the Starbucks and my friends surrounded me in excitement. My mom and Cori went to order our drinks while my other friend and I got seats. I looked over to see Cori and my mom tearing up and speaking quietly with each other. Once they joined us, there were tears shared and hugs exchanged, but then we moved on to other topics of life. It was a relief. Maybe things really would be able to get back to normal. Finally.

BACK TO CLASS

The next couple of days I prepared to go back to classes. My brother Michael had started attending the same college so it worked out that he could drive and help me with my books. Matt worked at my college and he offered to be there for anything that I needed. The day finally came for classes to start and I got dressed for my first day back for the semester. I safety-pinned my pant leg up on the right side so that it didn't drag. I didn't want to shorten all of my pants because my plan was to get a prosthetic leg and I wanted to be able to wear them again. I decided I was going to tie a bow around "Fat Louie" because I knew people would stare, so why not give them something to really stare at? I also was a little eccentric and liked to be different, so honestly, I enjoyed the look of it.

Michael wasn't in all of my classes so he would walk with me and help me get seated. When his class finished, he would meet back up with me and help me to the next class. After a while of doing this, though, I got more comfortable on my crutches. I found that I could actually carry my books in my backpack and get to my classes just fine. Michael did continue to accompany me to make sure I got there all right. I truly believe that he just wanted to protect me from anyone who might be rude or make a comment. He was my ultimate defender.

He's always been incredibly protective of his siblings, and I feel there is an especially strong bond between the two of us. Since all this happened, he has struggled with his faith and walk with God. Many years after this tragic experience, we were having an incredibly deep conversation, both crying because we felt such a negative shift in our relationship. We had once been best friends, but our relationship had declined to where we didn't know each other really at all. I felt like every conversation we had was either shallow or upsetting to him, because of my passion for Jesus. He told me that it's so hard for him to believe in a God who would allow his sister, someone who was so undeserving of this fate, to experience such a great loss. He basically screamed out the words, "Why would anyone serve such a cruel God?!"

We wept together and embraced. I had no idea that what I saw as a testimony of God's unfailing love and grace, Michael saw as a devastating series of events. I told him how much I loved him and that he was such a vital person in my story and forever will be. I told him that God is not an unloving God, but that sometimes in order to make the biggest impact, you have to go through some big loss. To this day, Michael and I disagree on many things, but we love each other unconditionally. He recently married the woman of his dreams, and I got to stand up there with them, knowing that Michael will always be one of my most cherished souls.

As I stuck to my heavy class schedule, I was still on pretty intense pain medication. I have no idea how I passed any of my classes—especially Italian. I don't remember anything but *ciao* and *pantalones!* This was upsetting because I had been really excited about that class. It was insane to think that it had been only a little more than two weeks since I had been in the hospital for HSP, and about a week and a half since I had lost my leg. I stuck close to my brother and my group of friends, and Matt would join me on his lunch break. I enjoyed being around others and making them laugh by dancing around on my crutches. Everyone was so nice; I would smile as people passed in the hallway, and honestly no one made me feel disabled or different. I had previously been working at the tutoring center as the receptionist and they welcomed me back with open arms. The tutors were so kind. However, they would pick on me about how fast and loud I was at typing. They never really talked about my amputation or asked how I was doing in that area of my life, which I appreciated because I just didn't want to dwell on it. I wanted to get back up and running into the next season of life, leaving this current season in the dust. I didn't want to be viewed as disabled; I was still very much me.

The only time my leg came up in conversation was when my crutches would fall on people by accident. As I sat at my desk, I leaned my crutches up against the coat hanger behind me, and occasionally people would walk by and cause the crutches to come tumbling down on them. Those metal sticks were a little dangerous. After a couple of months with the peacock-feather duct tape, I decided it was time to change it. I bought some yellow "caution" duct tape and we would all laugh hysterically at the new crutches.

Another humorous story that I will forever remember is about a girl who would come in weekly for tutoring. We would often chat as I sat behind the front desk. One day, I ran into her at a friend's gathering, which was apparently the first time she had ever seen me outside of work. She was a little taken aback and said to me, "Oh my gosh! I had no idea! What happened?" To which I responded, "What do you mean...?" Her eyes traveled down to my leg. I then decided to be silly and start running around screaming, "Where did it go? *Who took my leg? What has happened to my leg?!*" I am pretty sure she did not find this funny and was probably more concerned that I had lost my mind! However, we actually had a really good talk afterward. I told her all that had just happened in my life. The years that we knew each other, we would talk about that first interaction and laugh about it, so I suppose it didn't traumatize her too greatly.

FINDING MY WAY

As the semester carried on, my Shakespeare final was coming up. We had the option to write a paper, create a PowerPoint, or submit a video of some sort. I had a passion for creating little films and parodies with Michael. I loved the challenge of creating the script, choosing the actors and costumes, and then once it was recorded, I loved editing. This project triggered my passion for film, so I knew that was the route I wanted to go! However, it would be my first film project without my leg. I was nervous about my ability, but I was going to try. I decided to do a video based on *A Midsummer Night's Dream* and title it *A Midsummer's Nightmare*. Very original, right? I cast my sister as Helena, myself as Hermia, my friend Ryan as Demetrius, Matt as Lysander, and Michael as literally every other character.

What could have been a complete slam on my confidence actually turned out to be an amazing and fun day of shooting and messing around. I submitted the video to my teacher, and she *loved it*. She gave me a generous grade of A+, and actually showed it to several staff members and to classes that came after mine. I initially wanted to dwell on the thought, *She is probably just being really nice because I lost my leg...You can't give a one-legged girl a B.* But I quickly told myself to get out of that headspace because, frankly, I knew the amount of work that went into that project. I truly believed my teacher saw that. My sister, who worked as a teacher at the college, later confirmed that my professor had only the highest praise for the video. She couldn't believe how I went above and beyond for the project. I was the only student who went the film route; everyone else submitted either a paper or a PowerPoint. She was greatly entertained.

As time went on, school was going well (I was passing my classes who knows how), Matt and I were dating, and things just felt perfect. Or as Dwight from *The Office* would say, it was "Perfektenschlage." We had found a prosthetic clinic that we planned to work with once my incision had healed. An amazing couple, Pete and Judy Dechat, offered to pay for my first prosthesis! This was a huge blessing to my family as I had been without insurance since I turned nineteen. When I was undergoing chemotherapy, we had a really amazing insurance that covered the entire cost for kids all the way up through age eighteen. Who would have thought that the failing donut shop would actually be a blessing? Because of the financial state it put our family in, we qualified for Virginia's FAMIS insurance, which freed my parents from a huge hospital cost. They were able to focus on their child, not on how they were going to afford keeping their child alive. I am telling you—there is a reason for everything that God allows.

Life was coming together. I felt strong, my endurance level grew, and I was able to get around much easier. Though there were definite limitations, I chose not to see them. I knew getting a prosthesis was going to make things a whole lot easier and I just needed to be patient. While I was waiting for that next step to happen, I decided it was time to attempt driving. I knew that even with a prosthetic I would need to drive with my left leg, so why not try to get comfortable with it sooner, rather than later? One day, Matt asked if I wanted to come over and have dinner with his family. I had tested out driving the day before, just in my neighborhood, but this was the real deal. I was going to do it. Though I was nervous, I knew I was already a good driver; I just needed to get accustomed to using the other side of my body. It took about fifteen minutes to really get a feel for it and then…*success!* I felt exuberant! What I could have allowed this loss to take away instead became a strength within me. I wasn't going to allow anything to limit me. I may have had to do things differently, but I was determined to figure out a way to get it done.

I don't know what you might be facing right now, dear reader, but I want to encourage you to find a modified way. Do not just give up! Do not give in! As you read further on, I am going to discuss some very serious obstacles that came up. However, I learned that the most powerful tool to overcome these obstacles is our mindset. Surround yourself with people who see you for more than your loss, for more than your disability. Find a way to make life happen! Life is far too beautiful to just sit back and let it pass you by. It's worth making the effort.

DANCING AGAIN

One of the most significant people in my life, someone who stood in the ring beside me and saw me for more than my loss, was my friend and choreographer from my theater days, Sarah Worman-Connell. Shortly before I lost my leg, I had performed in *A Little Princess* with my theater group and Sarah had been the choreographer. Later in life, Sarah and I would find ourselves meeting up at Agora, my favorite coffee shop in downtown Fredericksburg, to explode with excitement as we met to discuss this very book. We laughed at silly memories, lost track of time reminiscing over dances, and cried over God's goodness and sovereignty. You see, God knew I would need Sarah for the biggest comeback story I would ever experience. So, what did He do? He connected Sarah with my theater group for my very last show with the company! A family attending her church had dropped the idea into her head. She said that it was so insane how she even got the job. The interview didn't go over her teaching ability at all, which she thought was odd. But they loved her personality and hired her immediately. I worked very closely with her during the show as it wasn't a large cast.

Sarah told me that she was originally drawn to me because my personality was larger than life. Also, that I was willing to try anything and that I just reflected light. The feelings were mutual as I felt drawn to Sarah and her bold, straightforward personality. She knew how to speak in love while never sugarcoating the truth. I would need this when I started dancing again. When Sarah heard that I had lost my leg, she felt an immediate dread—not only because she was a parent herself and could not imagine her child having to go through something like this, but she related because she grew up dancing. She understood how dance could become someone's identity and therefore knew the potential of feeling lost without it.

When my world stopped spinning and I regained some stability after my surgery, I reached out to Sarah. I had hoped that maybe she could work with me and Matt to see if we could try a couple of dance moves. I knew that if anyone could get on board with helping me find myself through dance again, it was going to be her. Her response was, "I have an even better idea. My church is putting on an art festival and I want you to dance there." We got together that very week to discuss details. The festival was in February, and it was currently the end of November, only a couple of months after my amputation. Sarah knew the timeline was not ideal, but she was determined to get me in front of an audience. She presented a song that was very dear to her personally: "Held" by Natalie Grant. As we listened, emotions ran high as I attempted to hold myself together; if ever I felt a real connection with a song, it was in this moment.

Rehearsals began immediately. It was a constant battle of trial and error. Over coffee, Sarah told me of her numerous sleepless nights trying to work through the moves in her head, only to find that they didn't physically work when tried. At one rehearsal, Sarah exclaimed, "I do not understand how this is not working!" So, what did she do? She went and got some belts, and she and Matt tied up their right legs to try to understand the weight shift and capabilities. It was the absolute coolest thing anyone had ever done. And it worked! Sarah was able to process through the moves, and the dance was created with such beauty and grace. I was learning to dance before I was even learning to walk on two legs again.

On nights where frustration would creep in, Sarah, whom I often referred to as "Momma," spoke words of love and wisdom, but also the hard truths I needed to hear. I remember one rehearsal where she had come up with this really cool move: I would roll over onto Matt's back, extend my leg, and hold it. It was beautiful when we hit it, but that was only half the time. One night I just couldn't get it. I was frustrated with myself and doubted that I would be ready for the festival. Sarah looked me in the eyes and said, "Melissa, you are getting in your head. You have done this so many times, and I don't want you for one second to even consider giving up. You are doing more than most people can do with two legs. Shake it off and let's try this again." She never let me consider failure. She believed in me and was not going to let me start spiraling. She continued to believe in me on the days I couldn't believe in myself. It's important to find people who push you to keep going when you can't push yourself.

As the weeks went on, Sarah was a constant in my life. Matt and I were over at her house four or five times a week. Her kids would run around us while we practiced, and I loved how involved her entire family was in the process. We would often finish up rehearsal and then stay to watch a movie or chat for hours. Sarah helped me to heal. Though she didn't know it at the time, her desire to get me back onstage was pivotal to my restoration. I don't think either of us had any idea the bigger picture of what God was about to do. The day of the art festival arrived quickly and I fought myself on feeling underprepared. But there I was, backstage with Matt and Sarah, costume on, and one lonely ballerina slipper on my left foot. I was not at all sure what to expect once our number was called. My nerves were running wild, but we prayed and gave the dance to our Lord.

Three. Two. One. The music began. We entered the stage. The lights on us felt hot and bright, almost aggressively bright. I could feel the audience holding their breaths in anticipation. But then, peace. Peace of the purest form. I felt like this performance had a spotlight coming down from heaven, like God was watching in excitement. I took a deep breath and let my emotions pour out, felt the weight of each word being sung. I was dancing in front of an audience, and I knew:

This would not be the last time.

CHAPTER SIX

GRIEF IS NOT THE ENEMY

My mom told me that after the dance as Matt carried me down the steps of the stage, the man sitting beside her leaned over and asked, "What happened? Is she okay? Did she hurt herself during the dance? Why is he carrying her?" My mom explained to him that I had only one leg and that Matt was helping me down the stairs because I didn't have my crutches. He was shocked to learn this because he hadn't noticed when I was dancing. He had no idea I was missing a leg! When I heard this, it made me want to cry. I was able to dance and not be seen simply as an amputee. My life after this first dance was unlike anything I could have expected or fathomed. I had the opportunity not only to continue dancing at other events and churches, but also to speak in various places. I could not believe that a small-town girl like me was getting to share my story with so many people. A few of my best friends on a competition dance team presented a whole dance about cancer. They competed in my honor and were even planning to wear a bow on their right thighs, just as I had done immediately after the amputation, but decided against it. It does looks a little bit more "sensual" when you have two legs.

My story was spreading. I had the opportunity to interview with local newspapers and even had a few YouTube interviews with reporters in Fredericksburg. I still cannot believe the doors God has opened. In 2020, I was given the huge honor of speaking on the "Make Life Matter" podcast, hosted by Angela Donadio, a successful author and friend. I had no idea how many people would hear my story, but right before my interview, Angela announced her podcast had officially hit over 20,000 downloads—many from out of the country and all over the world! I was in complete awe of my God. He has not stopped using me ever since I first put on a ballerina slipper and tulle skirt, and I feel humbled to say the least.

After "Held" became a statement piece in my life, the following years contained a whole lot of amazing, beautiful, complicated, and heartbreaking things. Let me share some of them with you.

RESTORING WHAT WAS LOST

The process for getting a prosthestic was a completely new world with unfamiliar twists and turns thrown our way. As I mentioned, once I turned nineteen I was no longer insured—and a prosthestic was not cheap. We found Hanger Clinic Prosthetics and Orthotics, and they would forever change my life. I had become used to crutches and could get around pretty well, but I missed the use of my hands. I wanted to walk again, to be able to live life more freely. When we found the Hanger Clinic, and they walked us through the process during our first appointment, I was so excited. I knew that they would carry me into the next season of my life. We talked about pricing and how I didn't have insurance, and they made us aware of the *little* wiggle room they could offer financially. It was a difficult conversation. The clinic did everything in their power to be gracious with the cost, but the pricing for the temporary prosthetic leg was still going to be around $7,500. This would not be my permanent prosthestic as it had a hydraulic knee with a rod going down to the foot. This allowed walking but didn't provide any knee resistance when walking up or down hills. But figuring out the finances for this temporary leg was a big ordeal.

As a family, we began praying for God's provision. We spoke to our church community about our needs and asked them to join us in prayer. In His perfect timing and love, we had an incredible family reach out to us. As I mentioned earlier, they wanted to completely cover the cost for this first prosthetic limb! The husband, Pete Dechat, had been through a tragedy of his own that God had brought him through. He and his wife, Judy, wanted to help me get through my loss as well. They didn't even know at the time that they were playing such a huge part in my story. The Dechats would spark something in me to reach a bigger group of people who had gone through incredible loss. So many people are out there, broken, afraid to grieve. Some may even feel that it shows a lack of faith. You need to know that God can restore all that is lost. I strongly encourage you to pick up a copy of Pete's book, *Through the Fire*, because you need to hear this man's story. He has strongly encouraged mine.

As I ambled into my appointment on crutches to get measured for my first prosthetic, Matt and my mom walked beside me. The room was filled with nervous excitement, everyone unsure of what all exactly this would entail. Daniel Mejia was my prosthetic clinician. He made me feel welcome and at ease and was quick to make me laugh. He told me that if I brought in a T-shirt with an image or logo that I liked, they could imprint it onto the socket of the prosthesis. I thought that was so cool. I promptly chose a cute Hello Kitty T-shirt, which would be updated to Perry the Platypus from *Phineas and Ferb* as soon as I got a different socket. When the appointment was over and we left, I knew it wouldn't be long before I would be up and going again. I was determined to be a fast learner and a brilliant walker, and by God's grace, I would even one day dance with my prosthetic leg.

LEARNING TO WALK AGAIN

It was finally the day! We had received the call that my prosthetic was ready to go, and we could pick it up. We called the Dechat family and they met us at the clinic. Matt had to work but would come over right after to help me practice walking. To assist in learning to walk again, we had made an appointment with Children's Hospital of Richmond Therapy Center. This is where I would have weekly physical therapy appointments. Everything was in line to get me walking on two legs again. I entered the office, with pure glee anticipating that this is where I would leave my crutches behind (though not literally, as I still needed to have them for days I was home and just milling around). But as I went through the process of putting on the liner and then the prosthetic leg, panic arose in me. It hurt. This wasn't what I had expected at all. My skin felt so sensitive and itchy in the liner. Daniel explained that this was usually the case and it would go away as my skin got used to being encased in a foreign product. But I hated it.

I was so disappointed. I had hoped to be forever rid of my crutches, but I was ready to get that clunky, heavy, itchy thing off me and run straight back into the arms of those annoying sticks. I tried to refrain from crying. I needed to believe that it would get better, plus the Dechat's were blessing me with this gift—the gift of walking—and I didn't want to come across as unthankful. But internally I was battling anger, not wanting anyone to know how angry I was, not even God (as if He didn't already know). Everyone kept saying how insanely brave and strong I was being. But I was frustrated that this amazing gift, which I thought was going to change my life in big ways, was not at all what I thought it would be. I didn't feel brave or strong.

As we left Hanger Clinic, I decided not to wear my leg. I hobbled defeatedly out of the building on my crutches, with my mom in front of me, carrying the hunk of metal, all the while the face of Hello Kitty staring back at me. She placed it in the trunk of the car, and we proceeded home. Upon arrival, she opened the trunk and we burst out laughing. There was the prosthetic leg, peaking out of the trunk with just the foot sticking out. What a bizarre sight! So we took a photo of it. We laughed for a good chunk of the day about it, and when Matt came over, we showed him the photo. I told him about how painful it was to wear the prosthesis and how defeated I felt. He told me he really wanted me to try it on and for us to practice walking, even just for a little bit. I fought him only slightly on this, because he was being so encouraging and reminding me of the goal: to walk again. To have use of my arms again. To no longer be confined to short distances.

We went down to my basement, which had been transformed into a dance room by the "Make a Wish Foundation," and I put my leg on. Holding onto Matt for dear life, we video recorded my first steps, then posted it to the YouTube channel we had created for my dance videos. The last I checked, that video has had over 63,000 views! To think that 63,000 people watched my second attempt of wearing a prosthetic limb truly blows my mind. That nineteen-year-old had no clue what her future would bring because she put that prosthesis on a second time. I have to give it to Matt for being a great encourager. God always knows what people we will need at the exact moment we will need them, even if it's just for a season.

You read that correctly; Matt is no longer a part of my life. God sent me a dance partner, but not my life partner. Matt helped me through the most tragic period of my life, but as time went on, the dynamic of our relationship changed. As individuals, we were changing. One of the biggest red flags that I wish I had seen was that I hadn't worked through my grief. I can honestly say I thought I was fine in the moment. I didn't even think about the loss of my leg for a really long time. I was improving in my walking ability and was finally wearing my prosthetic leg every day. It was a journey, and a hard one to say the least, but I had an amazing support group backing me the entire way. Because of all the positivity and growth I was feeling in my life, I was completely ignoring something very important: I had lost a leg. Whenever I would begin to process the loss and start to feel pain, I would push it back and think, *I am stronger than that feeling! It will not ruin my day!* What I didn't realize, though, was that it wasn't weakness to acknowledge that loss; it wasn't defeat to let it rush over my body and to *deal* with it. Grief was *not* my enemy.

However, delaying the grieving process for years to come would put a lot of strain on relationships that meant the most to me, as I was about to learn.

A SOLO DANCE

Physical therapy had been going well, but both my PT and I were ready for a more efficient knee. Time was rolling around for me to get my second prosthesis: a high-end, computerized gizmo called a "C-leg." I had been getting by on the "peg leg" but was so ready for this upgrade. Daniel had been telling me about all the things the C-leg would allow me to do, and I was beyond amazed. The knee, being an actual computer, would create resistance or lock when the heel was down, but when you shifted your weight to the toes, it would unlock and bend. It would be great for going up and down the sidewalk to our house. Also, it was going to change my life when going down the stairs. Though I would still have to go up the stairs one leg at a time (I called this "the Granny," with no offense intended to grandmothers!), my knee would create just enough resistance to comfortably go down the stairs normally. This would take me pretty much nine years to master, but now I am a total pro (or at least I think I am). Daniel also wanted to change my socket style to one that didn't require a liner, a much more modern way of doing things.

Despite all the excitement this brought me, I knew that there was no way the leg was going to happen until we raised the funds. Before we could start a GoFundMe page, or even chat with our church, something miraculous happened. Something had already been in the works, pretty much since we had gotten my temporary leg. A long-time friend of mine from dance, Emily McKinney, had begun putting together a big fundraising event—

all under my nose! I had absolutely no idea that for weeks on end she had been choreographing, scheduling rehearsals at our old dance studio, and speaking with different organizations in order to raise money. The venue was not to be used for fundraising events, but for some reason, they completely waived that rule. This allowed Emily to not only fundraise at the event but sell tickets. Em didn't stop there. She also created a checking account for a medical fund in my name and money was already flowing into it from various contributors.

The only thing I was aware of was that Sarah wanted to choreograph two dances for a talent show. She gave me the dates that we needed to have everything done by. She was determined to have me do a solo, something I was very unsure I could do. I fought her on it, just a little...maybe a lot. I was working with a very low-grade prosthetic leg, and we knew that it wasn't time for a dance with it. But dancing without the prosthesis or a partner would mean entering a completely new realm of problem solving. I relied heavily on Matt. A solo made me feel vulnerable and unworthy of being on stage. Because when you think about it, a dance is only half about the dancer; it's also about keeping the audience entertained. I wouldn't be able to leap around the stage and do countless pirouettes, but would have to rely on a lot of floor work. Sitting. On. My. Bottom.

When Sarah and I recently caught up, she finally expressed her fear at the time that people would not be impressed or entertained. She knew they would enjoy it because I was on stage doing what I loved the most, though she had absolutely no clue what she was going to do with me. Then the choreography came to her. I had told her the song I wanted to do my first solo to—it was "Dream" by Priscilla Ahn. After long nights of pondering, she saw the dance come to life in her head. During the first run-through of the entire dance, we laughed and cried because we both felt a lot of pride and joy in what we had created. My first solo! This dance wasn't for the crowd; this dance was for me.

Years later, sitting across from Sarah, I told her how that dance would show me I was strong enough to not have to rely on a dance partner. To not rely on anyone to get me through my life, other than my Lord and Savior. I could be an independent individual. That solo proved to me that what was about to happen in that season of my life was going to be okay. Even though I may not have felt strong in that moment, I was going to be fine. I didn't need a partner in order to find success or make it into adulthood. Although there is such beauty in having a partner, another person is never designed to heal you or fill a void. When you go through a tragedy, support is a blessing, but in the end it's between you and God. A person can't and won't fix you; only God can.

SOME SERIOUS ISSUES

To say I wasn't selfish in this time of my life would be an absolute lie, and I was very much focused on what I wanted. I hadn't dealt with or processed through anything that had happened; I just took it as it was. But resentment and anger were working their way up into the center of my heart. I started being the one thing that I absolutely cannot stand: *entitled*. Ugh, even typing that word is absolute horror to me. But entitlement reared its ugly head. I was constantly fighting Matt and my family on decisions, nitpicking every little thing, really lacking any respect for other people and their needs. Matt and I were both young, already in a difficult season where we were trying to figure out who we were, so that alone added a lot of pressure. We were trying to find our purpose. We were also just changing in general. We wanted different things out of life, and they weren't lining up. What we thought was an unbreakable bond was actually a false sense of stability brought on by undergoing a traumatic experience together. Our time together began to resort to awkward silence, and we both knew the end was coming.

The show was quickly approaching and the rehearsals with Matt and I began to feel just as awkward as we felt on the inside. But we didn't tell others what was going on between us. Not until the night before the benefit show. As we sat stretching on the floor at dress rehearsal, emotions were high. Matt had expressed to me the night before that he felt we needed to take a break. You may be thinking, *Why on earth would he do that right before a huge show?* Well, like I had said, things had been pretty rough for a while. We have to give grace to those two kids who were so far from being ready to deal with such adult things. So, with that being said, he let me know his thoughts and I basically lost it. I was so upset with him. But even more so I was just entirely crushed. I didn't understand why this was all happening. I could't see God in it at the time. I was in a very dark and low mental state. Matt didn't know how to help me because he wasn't the one who could. I didn't know how to go to the One who could help me because I didn't know there was even a problem!

So there we were, in the dark room of the venue where we would be performing the next day, with Sarah, stretching and preparing to practice our "couples" dance. We couldn't hide how we were feeling. Matt resorted to shutting me out, basically ignoring me. I resorted to glaring and basically crying the entire time we stretched. Sarah had had enough. She looked us both straight in the eyes and said, "You both need to quit this right now. I know you guys are working through some things, but you have to complete this show. This can't happen right now. You guys were dating when this started, and you have to complete it. You guys need to get your heads back in the game." She also pointed out that when you can't trust your dance partner, people end up getting hurt.

So, we were reminded to get our act together. You may think that was kind of harsh but I couldn't have thanked Sarah more for that moment. She reminded us that this show wasn't about us; it wasn't about our personal issues. It was about the people involved, the hard work that had gone into this, the people who had sacrificed so much of their time and money to make it happen. It was about the audience who would be impacted, the families who had gone through loss, and the people who had suffered through their own disabilities. It wasn't about me and Matt. The show had to go on.

THE LAST DANCE

The benefit show was named "Roses Are Yellow." Instead of the typical saying "Roses Are Red," Em wanted to evoke the idea that we can be a little bit out of the norm and still be beautiful and accepted. The show consisted of twenty-one acts, all pertaining to different disabilities. Emily choreographed the dances in such a beautiful way. She also had a few of my friends sing different songs from some of my favorite Broadway shows at that time. At one of the early rehearsals, Emily wanted everyone to experience how it was for me when I danced. She had everyone tie up their leg and try to do their dance routine. Many stumbled or fell but she wanted them to know the feeling, to be able to evoke that emotion. It was also a way for the group (all of whom were my friends) to deal with the emotions they were processing with my loss.

Emily herself knew great pain and loss in her life as she had suddenly started experiencing seizures in her sophomore year of college. We had met when we were children in dance and have pushed each other since day one. We would critique each other in the most loving way, and I truly owe a lot of my passion for dance to Emily. However, when she started having seizures in college (and one of the reasons she was in school was for dance), her dreams were radically put on hold. She suddenly faced many limitations with no way out in sight. In her worst season, she was having up to two hundred seizures a day. On the nights that she would lie awake in bed, wondering if she would wake up in the morning, she would choreograph in her head. The next time she had an opportunity to dance, she would express all of her emotions out on the floor. She expressed that she truly believed dance saved her. It gave her an outlet to communicate with her body and express her pain without having to actually talk about it. So she got it; she understood how I felt. By putting on this benefit show for me, she was giving me an outlet to dance, a way to express my emotions and hurt. Without her even knowing that I was processing through some big shifts in my life, she was giving me the opportunity to dance it out.

Just like that, it was showtime. Sarah glided backstage in her Guess high heels to give us our pre-performance pep talk. She informed us that the venue was so packed that people were having to stand. This was it; Matt and I knew this might be our last dance together, which put a lot of weight on the performance. Per the conversation we had the night before, we knew we had to put all the chaos aside and have fun. That is what Sarah reminded us—to have the time of our lives out there. We took a group photo (which Sarah and I feel is one of our favorite photos of us), I removed my leg warmer, and Matt carried me up the back stairs to the stage. We got ourselves into position and the show started.

Our dance together was to the song "I Don't Dance" by Frank Sinatra, using the remixed version from the movie *Step Up 3*. We literally had the time of our lives, and when he flipped me up into a lift called the "blue bird" the crowd went wild. I even did the "worm" at one point. We finished the dance and received a standing ovation. The applause was unreal; the room was so packed that it felt like the walls shook. I wanted to cry—what an experience! There was one number in particular that my friend Cori and Emily's brother Matt performed to the song "Fix You" by Coldplay. The dance was about a girl who had cancer, and there was not one dry eye in the room. Cori wore a beautiful head scarf, and as they danced through the pain, you felt each emotion. When they finished the dance, they embraced and he carried her off the stage. It was such a beautiful piece and stunningly choreographed. But it awoke pain in me that I hadn't felt in a very long time. Tears filled my eyes as I fought to shove those feelings back down. That day was not to be the day that I dealt with the emotions that accompanied losing my leg.

The day after the first show, it felt so surreal knowing that both shows were sold out. Seeing the number of people who came through for this event was astonishing. The sacrifice of time that was put in by all the dancers, the selflessness of everyone—doing all of this just for me—humbled me greatly. It was also amazing to see other dance studios sending their love, as they donated almost two hundred pointe shoes! Em not only used these shoes as decorations on the stage but decorated each one uniquely. At the show they were sold and the profits went toward my medical fund. After the first night, Emily checked the bank account she had set up and found that $12,000 had been raised, just from that one show! That wasn't even including the profits from concessions and pointe shoes, and we still had one more performance to go! That benefit show alone covered the cost for my new prosthetic leg. So, say it with me:

Miracle. Working. God.

CHAPTER SEVEN

EMOTIONAL OVERLOAD

The weekend of the benefit show concluded, and we had made well over the goal to be able to get my new prosthetic leg. We actually raised enough to keep up with repairs for the next couple of years! I was in complete awe of my God. I mean, how could I have even questioned His goodness? He had never failed me, and He wasn't going to start now. I love reading Matthew 6:25–34, which truly lays out some serious love and provision. Get ready for some poetic truth:

> "Therefore I tell you, do not worry about your life, what you will eat or drink; or about your body, what you will wear. Is not life more than food, and the body more than clothes? Look at the birds of the air; they do not sow or reap or store away in barns, and yet your heavenly Father feeds them. Are you not much more valuable than they? Can any one of you by worrying add a single hour to your life?

"And why do you worry about clothes? See how the flowers of the field grow. They do not labor or spin. Yet I tell you that not even Solomon in all his splendor was dressed like one of these. If that is how God clothes the grass of the field, which is here today and tomorrow is thrown into the fire, will he not much more clothe you—you of little faith? So do not worry, saying, 'What shall we eat?' or 'What shall we drink?' or 'What shall we wear?' For the pagans run after all these things, and your heavenly Father knows that you need them. But seek first his kingdom and his righteousness, and all these things will be given to you as well. Therefore do not worry about tomorrow, for tomorrow will worry about itself. Each day has enough trouble of its own." (NIV)

Not only will He never stop providing for our needs, but there are hundreds of mentions of His love throughout the Old and New Testaments. He is the very definition of love. God could not be more clear about how He cares about us and desires that we be in close connection with Him. Zephaniah 3:17 tells us,

The LORD your God is in your midst, a Warrior who saves. He will rejoice over you with joy; He will be quiet in His love [making no mention of your past sins], He will rejoice over you with shouts of joy. (AMP)

How great our heavenly Father loves us, how deeply He treasures us. He rejoices over us! As the rollercoaster of my life continued, He would shower me in His lovingkindness consistently, even if sometimes I would choose not to acknowledge it. He would rejoice over me in the little things, in the big events, and in every waking moment.

LIFE ON MY OWN

After a two-week break, Matt and I met to talk about our relationship. We decided we needed to say goodbye. We had been trying to make the best of something that had ended awhile before it actually, physically ended. A lot of people ask me why Matt and I didn't stay in touch or try to remain friends. My personal opinion is that it was healthier for us both to just say goodbye. Because he had been through one of the most tragic experiences in my life, I had become dependent on finding my confidence through Matt, and the moment that I had to rely on myself it was incredibly eye opening. For a long time, because I was so used to relying on Matt, I would grasp onto anyone close to me and transfer my dependency onto them. I remember the first hard conversation with my friend, Cristy, about the dependency she was seeing. There were times when she would walk really fast ahead of me so I wouldn't use her as a walking stick. She felt that I relied too much on her, and some of my other friends, to simply function in life. I remember getting so mad and offended at her that we didn't talk for a whole day (which was very unusual for us). But then I prayed about what she said and I realized she was completely hitting the nail on the head. I was petrified of doing anything on my own. Even in decision-making I relied heavily on my parents. Sometimes it's those ugly conversations that open your eyes the most to the hard reality of your blindspots.

LIMITS LEFT AND RIGHT

It was strange going to my appointment to receive my new prosthetic leg without Matt. The excitement was there, but I was so used to his encouragement that it was weird trying to pump myself up. When I tried the prosthesis on, lots of adjustments had to be made because I was turning into a bit of a difficult case. Because I was an AK (above knee) amputee, "Fat Louie" was pretty fleshy and, might I just say, squishy. This made it hard to shape a socket that had a snug fit but didn't rub me the wrong way. I still had four muscles in my leg, so working really hard to keep them toned helped somewhat, but not much. However, with the new "suction cup" socket, I wouldn't have to wear a silicone liner; it would therefore be truer to size and fit more snugly. We had hopes that this might be the answer to the fit issues.

To make this work, I had to put something that looked like a trash bag over my leg and pull it through a hole at the bottom of the socket. That is probably hard to envision, but it was literally just that: a blue "trash bag" used to slip the skin into the socket. I was so excited for this new approach and, even better, they were able to put a cover on the prosthetic. They had sent it off to a specialist with measurements and a photo of my left leg, and there they shaped it out of foam and covered it with "skin" so it matched my other leg. (Side bar: My shade was *zero* as I am practically translucent.) I liked having a cover because it filled out my jeans. All was going well! I felt that the appointment was a huge success. I was walking pretty easily in the new leg and all of us, including Daniel, were shocked at how quickly I was adjusting. But then there was the car ride home. My skin was very sensitive and wasn't used to the lining of the socket, so it was itching *so bad* that I was on the verge of crying.

When we got home, I rushed inside and sat on our steps and began to cry. As soon as my mom got inside, I yelled, *"Get it off. Get it off!"* I sobbed to my mom as if I were completely incapable of removing it. I remember at that point it also felt *so tight*. My mom walked past me and said, "Melissa, get your attitude together.

You're completely capable of removing your prosthetic." That's some momma truth right there. I immediately stopped crying, literally turning off the water works in a mere second. What was with this toddler persona I was putting on? Realizing my foolishness, I pressed the button that released the suction and I removed the prosthetic, revealing a very purple "Fat Louie."

What I wasn't seeing at the time was that my mindset was beginning to shift. All the positivity I had felt was starting to be less of a constant companion in my mind and more like a guest that popped in occasionally. I had been given so many opportunities, even the opportunity to write this book back at age nineteen. But I praise and thank Jesus that I didn't write it then, because it would have amounted to mere fluff and empty words that I thought sounded nice. You see, I was about to go through a very pivotal moment in my story. If I had written this book before that season, I wouldn't have been able to offer what my heart desires to offer you today. I wouldn't have been able to speak from the truest place in my heart and share the darkest times in my life—and the incredible victory that I experienced, only because I serve such an incredibly loving God.

Before, when it seemed I had everything going for me, I didn't have a chance to really process through what had happened in my life. Immediately following the loss of my leg, I had a boyfriend, was surrounded by a great community, and was dancing regularly. People wanted me to come to their churches and speak. People *wanted* me. I was told that I was so strong, that I had an amazing story to be told, that I was literally unstoppable. But on the inside I didn't feel strong, I didn't feel unstoppable; if anything, I felt like I was being hit with limits left and right. I knew God's plan was higher than mine and that I hadn't been completely forgotten.

However, I was struggling with processing even the idea of the possibility that maybe I was dealing with grief—and I was ashamed. So I stuffed it down and thought I had been moving forward pretty effortlessly.

Then just like that, life took a turn and everything changed. Suddenly, it was like the fast pace of the previous year and a half was now a trudge. I was single, Sarah became busy with her life and kiddos and couldn't meet to dance as much, and there were no more offers of speaking events. I felt utterly alone. It gave me a lot of time to think. Unfortunately, this overthinking turned into wallowing in hurt and anger, which then turned into resentment, entitlement, brokenness, and a whole lot of mess. A lot of it. For a long time I felt entitled, I stayed broken, and I blamed other people for what was going on internally.

Eventually, there was a breakthrough. Not through my own doing, but through a sovereign God who wouldn't allow me to stay where I was, no matter how hard I pressed my feet into the mud. So, here we are, nine years after my amputation, and I am coming to you from a very vulnerable place. You're going to hear some ugly things about me, which I dread. But above everything else, I have to put aside the fear of what people might think in finding out I wasn't all together. I have to tell you what I learned. I have to tell you all the icky, gritty, crummy stuff because it would absolutely not be okay for me to keep what I have learned all to myself.

So, my dear reader, let's get muddy.

CHAPTER EIGHT

BUT FIRST, FORGIVENESS

Once my life came to a screeching halt, I started to dwell on the negative: *How in the world did I get the "honor" of being among the 1 percent to have the osteosarcoma return and steal my leg? Why was I so "unique"?* I began to have a lot of moments of angry prayers and hurt feelings toward God. I was just so confused. With Matt no longer in the picture, I turned to other people to tell me my worth and value, and they always fell short. Their words would never, and could never, be enough; they didn't have that power. But alas, I still continued to try to find my worth and purpose through people.

To say that I never played the victim card would be an absolute lie. There were days when I would be working out with friends, hiking, or simply walking downtown and I would get that hint of a whine in my voice. Then the thoughts would rush in: *They have no idea what it's like to be me. No one understands how much pain I'm in. They keep telling me to push harder and keep going but they don't feel the friction between my prosthetic and a nerve.* Resentment would start to grow. I would wallow in the "woe is me" mental space. It made my testimony weak for a season. I would share what God had done for me, talk about how He used my dad to change my mindset, but on the inside I felt anger. I felt selfish. What was worse, I felt justified in how I felt. The funny thing is, dark places can never stay hidden from the light for long. I was only so good an actress, but God is the director, and I wasn't selling the act to Him.

To add to the mental battles I was facing, the physical struggles increased. I was having a lot of issues with my prosthetic. The suction socket wasn't working for me because if I sweated the least amount, the leg would start to come off. It was also agitating the top of my leg quite a bit, and it would take some time getting the right fit and padding. I was frustrated about the length of time it was taking to figure out my prosthetic, my walking, my life. I was hurting on both the outside and the inside but was still trying to stifle what I was really battling. I was trying to solve my problems, alone and ineffectively. Because I was in a dark headspace, situations that I hadn't previously noticed started to wear heavily on me. Judgmental glances, whispers, kids staring, and even worse, their parents gawking alongside them. There were a few situations that really left me feeling absolutely worthless.

My dad, one of my friends, Jaina, and I had attended a phenomenal Nationals baseball game (go Nats!). After a long walk back to the elevators, my prosthetic was genuinely rubbing my upper leg raw. It was so bad that I was almost to the point of tears and asking my dad to carry me. However, I was able to hobble and wobble my way to the elevator that would lead us to the level where our car was parked. We got to the crowded elevator and pressed our floor number. A woman behind us made a comment to her husband in a loud, snarky voice, "Wow, they couldn't take the stairs one floor?" I turned to her and, trying to remain kind, I said, "I'm sorry. I have a prosthetic leg and I'm having some issues with it hurting me right now." She then proceeded to whisper cruelties about me to her husband. I had the cover on my prosthetic so I am not sure if she believed me or not, but as soon as we got to our car I cried uncontrollably. My dad was about to run up the stairs to their floor but felt God impressing him to remain calm and just be there for me. He was grieving with me, and Jaina was in complete horror of the whole situation. I felt so raw both from the pain of my prosthetic and the pain I was feeling inside. How could someone be so absolutely horrible?

Jaina and I recently talked about this memory. I had actually forgotten about it and had put it to rest, but talking about it raised some ugly feelings inside of me. I found myself angry again at that woman, angry at her cruel attitude, even on the verge of wishing someone in her future would tell her off. Hours after Jaina and I had talked about it, I lay in bed dwelling on it, but then a word overwhelmed me: forgiveness. *Forgiveness.* As I spoke that word over and over, my body relaxed, I unfurled my brow, and peace fell. I realized I had never acknowledged forgiveness toward that woman, or any person who has made me feel less of a human. As I went through each instance and forgave those people, a fresh breath of air rose in me. I began to think of those who stared at the beach, in restaurants, even when I would be on the job working as a makeup artist and enjoying the gifts God gave me. To those people, I no longer felt bitterness, but release. I didn't even realize I had been holding onto such anger and hurt until that night, in 2020, after so many years of burying it. What power there is in forgiveness!

Forgiving, I discovered, was my first step toward real healing. I could not believe, as I lay in my bed in 2020, how many people I had written off, feeling disgusted toward them as human beings. I was holding offense toward them, and in return, I was the one losing sleep and growing in resentment. I showed no mercy or grace; I let hurt reside in the deepest parts of my heart and I was now stuck in that place. But so many years later, the memories came flooding back to my mind. I finally let go of all the hurt and resentment I had toward these people. This was a pivotal moment.

I also want to mention something that I have to remember regularly. Before you make a comment under your breath about someone, or you judge the person, remember that you don't know the full story. That woman at the Nats game couldn't tell I had a prosthetic leg, so she assumed that I was being lazy. We have to be bigger than our initial assumptions. If we go around just letting our minds control our opinion of people, where is the love? Where is the kindness? Where is Jesus in us? I have fallen short many a time, but who ever made me the judge? Who gave me that power? Judgment is such an ugly thing. Be self-aware enough to not make someone feel unworthy. If you have a question, *ask*, instead of just staring and whispering. I welcome questions! Come talk to me; have a conversation. I am developing thicker skin (something that God has been working with me on), and I would rather you know the full story instead of making assumptions. Let's get better in this area. Let's be better.

Be the reason people laugh or get to share a part of themselves. Don't be the reason they go home crying. No one deserves to be just an assumption.

JOY IN TIMES OF SORROW

It is amazing how, even in our dark seasons, God will still bring us laughter and joy. I think it's important to show how even through my moments of feeling utterly alone, God was still very much present, and might I say, He is quite the comedian.

In 2017, I was still working through my mess, but the day that my dad announced we would be going whitewater rafting, I was so excited. I had never been, because by the time I was old enough to do it, too much life had happened and it was no longer a family tradition. My dad, being the "modern hipster" he is, booked an amazing Airbnb in Pennsylvania and our family prepared for the trip. The only problem I was facing was that my C-leg could not get wet. I would need to go in and get a leg similar to my first temporary leg, something with a simple rod and hydraulic knee. Hanger Clinic didn't have a lot of time to prepare, so they put together something they had lying around in the shop. Unfortunately, they had to substitute my foot with a man's foot. I didn't really mind until I realized I couldn't fit my shoe on it. So, when we got to the river, I was rocking a single shoe. I had become so used to the resistance provided by my C-leg that walking with the "peg leg" again proved to be quite difficult. Not only that, but for some reason the foot had become slightly unscrewed and kept turning around as I walked. At several points, we would have to stop because my foot had turned completely backward. What a sight to be seen!

My brother Dan carried me a lot of the way, but I was a lot heavier than his little kiddos and ended up wearing him out. Once we got on the water, though, we had an absolute blast. My stomach was sore from laughing at all the funny commentary. It was a beautiful reminder of how phenomenal a leader my father is. He was our raft director. We had only one mishap where we were all thrown from the raft—frankly, because we didn't heed his guidance at one point. What an amazing example of our heavenly Father. He guides us flawlessly, gives us direction when we seek it, speaks clearly until we tune Him out, and yet, when we tumble out of the boat, He is quick to pull us back in. I had been afraid to fall out of the raft because of the drilled-in instructions, which were to keep your feet up and out of the water. This was how people drown, by getting their feet stuck in rocks. You are supposed to hold your feet up and let the water carry you until you can reach your raft again. But I was concerned my prosthetic would drag me down because of how heavy it was. I had come to terms with the idea that, if I fell out of the boat, I would potentially have to release my leg to the rushing waters. So dramatic.

When we hit the huge rock that caused those of us on the left side to topple into the right-side victims, I had my "Frodo and Sam" moment. I was under the water for what felt like forever, truly questioning if I needed to unstrap my leg and let it sink to the bottom. But then my dad grabbed my arm and pulled me up, with Dan quick to grab me and literally throw me back into the raft. We all laughed about how I was under the water for only a split second, and yet I was contemplating releasing that expensive piece of metal to the bottom of the river.

Another moment of pure laughter was when I had to send my prosthetic in to get a new cover put on it. I was meeting one of my friends, Casi, at the mall, so I was in a rush. Before I really checked if everything felt all right, I just said, "Looks good!" I walked into the mall with no issue, but minutes later I was standing in Charlotte Russe with Casi and something snapped. I took one step and immediately knew something was not right. Then after one more step, my prosthetic completely folded inward. It had to have been the most insane-looking thing for someone walking by to see. But the even crazier thing was that not one onlooker stopped to help. Casi and her little 120-pound self lifted me up like a bride and carried me to the closest bench. She then went on the search for a wheelchair. We were both crying from laughter and probably also a little from nerves. I couldn't believe that had just happened. She wheeled me out to my car, and I was on my way right back to Hanger. They fixed the problem quickly and I went back to meet Casi for coffee. What a day!

One last story that truly shed so much joy in such a dry season was when my brother Michael challenged me to a light-saber duel. You see, when he had been living with my parents, he used to have a group of friends come over weekly and have these huge lightsaber battles. I wouldn't admit it to him then, but it was actually pretty epic. On Michael's twenty-third birthday he invited his friends over for a special battle, and when I arrived at the house, all I could see in the dark evening were flashes of reds, blues, and greens. I went inside but secretly wanted to join in on the festivities. As Michael's friends started to leave, I went outside to talk to him. I was not expecting him to extend his lightsaber and challenge me to a duel. Before we called the rest of the family out to watch the battle, my dad, Michael, and I devised a plan. What only the three of us knew was that I had loosened the strap to my prosthetic so that when Michael "sliced" it with his lightsaber, it would fall off. The "audience" went crazy. We all laughed until we cried.

It was moments like these that helped me to forget my pain and questions of why. Laughter truly is medicine to a hurting soul. It is such a beautiful thing; it is such an important thing. I would even go so far as to say that laughing in times of great sorrow is incredibly necessary in order to start the healing, though it didn't completely solve the problem. Only one thing would:

Acknowledging there is a problem in the first place.

CHAPTER NINE

GROWING PAINS

Though I eventually discovered the power of forgiveness, it was only after years of wallowing in anger, hurt, and resentment. For years, I did not feel seen by God; quite frankly I felt forgotten. I welcomed the fact that He was a gracious God and would take care of me, but there was something in the back of my mind that was creeping closer to the front: bitterness. I was bitter toward Him, bitter that He chose me, and bitter that He put me in a position where, if I were to accept, He would send me to help others who had been through trauma and great loss. I was bitter to be chosen to have to live this out.

The bitterness extended toward the people I loved the most, and was reflected in how I treated people and how I felt about myself. I had so much resentment inside me that I was frustrated with my friends for being encouraging. When they would try to encourage me, while showing tough love when I would act defeated, I would argue by saying, "You don't know the whole story. You don't know my life, so you don't get to have a say in how I am choosing to live my life." I was getting angry because of the unresolved issues in my heart.

When you don't process through big changes in your life, it will only breed death; you will not be able to flourish. You have to process the trauma. If you don't, you will continue to make poor decisions. You will continue to hurt others because you are hurting. Even if you feel like you have healed and mended, if you haven't dealt with the grief and gotten to the root of the situation, that little weed is going to grow into a tree, which is much harder to pluck out. It will become so deeply rooted that you will not be able to uproot it alone. Only God, the master gardener, will be able to pluck it out with ease. This is a beautiful visual that my mom shared when we were recently speaking on the matter of our hearts. I had a rotten tree deeply rooted inside of me. It was so big and dark that it was overshadowing my day-to-day life, bleeding into my relationships.

What started as little disagreements here and there turned into constant friction as friends and family felt they had to walk on eggshells around me. I would pick little fights over the most irrational things. A prime example was one night when I was with a group of friends and we were playing a game outside. We were picking people for teams and Jaina said something about wishing she had Casi on her team, which for some reason made me feel incredibly small and insignificant. Such a little thing, right? Well, I blew it totally out of proportion and left the party early, as the lie of being rejected weighed heavily on me. I texted Jaina that night explaining how I was feeling and she immediately apologized and said that she had no intention of making me feel rejected. But that was just it—I believed that everyone was rejecting me. I wish I could say that at that moment I realized what I was doing and moved on without another look back. But no; I held onto my feeling that Jaina rejected me, and I began to ignore her texts or be snarky in my reply. I also would bring it up again and again, and finally she said, "Mel, I don't know what else you want from me. I have apologized and told you that I was not rejecting you." I did not respond. I wanted to feel like I was in control.

THE INTERVENTION

The next day Casi texted me to ask if I wanted to get coffee with her, Jaina, and Cristy. Casi had moved out of the state so I was all for a girls' hangout. I was excited about seeing everyone. We met at our usual spot and the girls climbed into my car as the rain poured down on that gray morning. I started talking to Casi and giving her updates on my life, not realizing that Jaina and Cristy were really quiet. Then Cristy suddenly spoke up, but instead of her usual calm demeanor, her voice was trembling and sad. She talked fast and I could tell she was afraid of being cut off. She told me that she was incredibly confused with my behavior and didn't feel safe around me anymore. There had been several instances in which I had lashed out at her for absolutely no reason and made her feel guilty. In moments where she had tried to challenge me to be better, to be stronger, I had gotten offended and told her that she just didn't understand. She expressed that she had tried for so long to extend grace but was struggling to know how to move forward in the relationship. She was tired of me isolating myself, but then turning it around on them and making them feel like they were the bad guys.

I was in complete shock. Cristy had always been the level one in our group, slow to anger and incredibly understanding. I knew that this was serious if she was speaking with such passion and fervency. It broke my heart hearing how I had hurt them so greatly and never even thought to apologize. My eyes began to tear…but it wasn't over. Years of hurt were about to be uncovered, laid out, and dealt with.

It was then Casi's turn. I had recently expressed to her how much I wanted to really work out and regain my strength and endurance. One day, Casi had texted me asking how my week had gone with working out. Granted, it had been a rough week; I had taken on more than I could handle workwise and was not finding any *me* time. But instead of relaying this to Casi, I flipped out on her. I told her that my career was far more important to me than the gym. I needed her to back off and understand that I wasn't "like her," and that I was tired of feeling guilt tripped. Casi was in utter confusion as I had asked her to keep me accountable. I think you're getting the idea of the horrible place I was in—and the awful friend I had become. Admitting this makes me feel sick to my stomach, but I have to share my whole story, and this just happens to be a really big part of it.

Lastly, all eyes turned to Jaina, who was on the verge of tears. She looked at me and just asked, "Mel, why are you pushing us away? What is happening?" Tears began to roll as I realized I had indeed been isolating myself, because I had made myself the victim and played that hand. I had decided that I would be the one to burn the bridge, not the other way around. Instead of people choosing that I wasn't worth their time, I was going to make them feel that pain. But here were these friends who had literally been through the fire with me, stood beside me in the good and the bad, and for some reason I had gotten it in my head that I was a burden to them, that my pain was too heavy and that they would eventually leave. I was believing an outright lie.

You see, one of the devil's biggest weapons is disunity—and I had fallen for it. I had isolated myself and believed that being alone was the best way to process my loss. My once united front had turned into just me, at least in my head. But these friends were not going to let me walk out of their lives without a good fight. There is power in numbers, and the devil knows that. When I was in South Africa for a missions trip, we went on a safari. The tour guide was driving us through where the lions were, explaining to us how they hunt. Lions wait for their prey to fall behind, become injured, or get lost, separating it from the safety of others. Then once it is alone, they pounce and bam, they have their KFC family dinner. The devil has the same mindset. When you are alone with your thoughts, isn't it so much harder to feel strong? To feel like you have yourself together? Don't you notice little lies popping up, even if they seem small and irrelevant?

Really think about that for a second. A lot of people battle depression, especially when winter comes. What do you notice happens? Isolation. Isolation breeds depression, and if you don't catch it in time, you're sucked in and just want to remain bedridden. Isolation doesn't always involve staying in bed, though. I was among my friends constantly yet was emotionally distant. I didn't share my thoughts as much and tended to be more guarded with my responses. Despite seeming joyful and having a smile on my face, I didn't want anyone to know my real thoughts, the really dark and gunky ones. This left me feeling like I had all this weight on my shoulders, a literal heaviness that you won't really understand unless you've gone through it—which I hope that you don't. But God always knows what you're going through, in those long nights with covers drawn over your head and a heaviness in your chest. He also knows the people who are going to help you carry that weight.

DEALING WITH THE ROOT

I will never be able to thank my friends enough for being bold. They knew a shift had happened in me and instead of just letting me walk myself out of their lives, they decided something had to be said and an intervention was needed. They were not going to give up on me. I will never forget Cristy's anxious tone as she tried to stand her ground and still extend grace. So many tears were shed in that car in the Starbucks parking lot, but breakthrough was also found. The girls listened as I had the revelation that I had been pushing them away out of fear of rejection. That rejection had been the bully I had faced ever since I was a child.

They listened as I tearfully apologized for abusing their friendships and I told them how much they truly meant to me. They listened as I began to finally process the grief of losing my leg and accept that it was a reality I needed to deal with. Be thankful for the people who don't let you sit in your ruins. Is it awful and brutal in the moment? Yes, it most definitely is. When those who love you enough to boldly tell you what they are seeing, don't shun them; instead, you need to embrace those people for all they are. Praise God for them. Praise God for friends who are bold even when it means they could lose someone they love.

As I was asking Cristy questions so I could accurately write this section, she commented, "With grief, you never get over it; you learn to live with it. When you watch a friend go through great loss, you don't want to keep identifying a hard season that they're having with past trauma. You also don't want to disregard that they could still be bleeding out from that loss. You need to have people in your life who will be honest with you while extending you grace, who can honestly ask you, 'Where is this stemming from?' Is it something from past hurt or do we need to dig deeper for another root? We can never know exactly what you've gone through, we can't know the pain, but every human can identify when there is a root that hasn't been dealt with. The branches can't be figured out until the roots are dealt with. There has to be grace—grace for us, and grace for you. You have to know when to extend grace, or when it's time to actually address the problem and bring it to the light."

I. Needed. To. Grieve. Grieving is not a sin; it is realistic and healthy. I, Melissa Eadie, had indeed suffered a great loss. No doubt about it, no shame about it. It was a fact. But my story was still very much in God's hands, and I was strong, and I had been through a lot for a kid. I still sometimes feel like that kid waking up in a hospital room, losing a part of her. I had to acknowledge that and grieve my loss. I learned that grief doesn't mean you're not trusting God. I believe that God grieves with us! Psalm 56:8 says that God keeps our tears in a bottle. He treasures them because our hurts matter to Him. I needed to stop asking God, "Why?" and start asking Him, "All right, how do I proceed?" Stop asking God, "Why did You choose me?" Start asking, "How would You like to use me?"

I still sometimes cry over the loss of my leg. The loss will always be there; after all, I have a visual reminder every day. But it's the mindset behind the tears that is different. I have cried out to God to change me from the inside out, to make me stronger in Him. To show me how to be courageous and kind in all things, to love and extend grace. To be willing to go where He says, "Go," and to stay when He says, "Stay." God is the ultimate author—He doesn't leave out one single detail. He doesn't allow the impact of grief into our lives so He can then just drop us. I may not have always been aware of it, but He was molding me into a warrior.

Trusting in God and choosing to live for Him doesn't insulate us from heartbreak. Sometimes the simple choice to follow Him actually brings a whole new set of heartbreak. But please remember within your trials that this doesn't mean God has forgotten you or that He neglected to give you a purpose. Actually, it is reason to believe that you were chosen *for such a time as this*. Remember, we also are in constant battle with the devil. He wants you. He wants to see you break, to watch you cave under the weight. But it's because he knows you have great purpose. He knows that God has a specific plan for you, and he fears that you will process through the loss and won't remain in the pit of darkness for long.

Reader, I have to inform you of something awful. The devil hates you; he really despises you. However, he is also afraid of you because of the God in you. He knows that every lie he whispers to you is simply that: a lie. So when you hear the words, "God did this. He doesn't love you," you speak right back to that voice, "Nope! God loves me; I am highly favored, highly adored. Jesus will bring beauty from this! You have no place here. Leave me alone!" When you hear, "I am not enough," you speak right back to that voice, "I am enough! I am an heir of the King of kings! He calls me his own!" The Word of God is truth, so when you are hit with a lie, cover yourself in truth. You were made for greater things, my dear friend. So *be bold*. Even with great loss, you are made for great purpose.

If everything is taken away, but you can still worship and glorify the Lord, was anything really taken away?

—*Casi Briggs*

CHAPTER TEN

MEANT TO BE SENT

I cannot believe that it took almost nine years for me to work through my grief, to recognize what had grown so deep inside of me. If you get anything out of reading this book, I hope that it will help you to process any bitterness, grief, or anger far faster than I did. Even though I wish I had worked through everything sooner, I am thankful that it was revealed to me through people I love and that, by the grace of God, it was even brought to my attention at all in this lifetime. Some people never find release from their pain and sorrow, and eventually it turns into a great numbness. Knowing this, I have never been more thankful for God's abundant grace through several seasons of growth. Acknowledging and *feeling* the grief led to breakthrough and release from the consistent ache of loss.

I also feel the need to mention that there is no shame in the amount of time it takes to work through and process the loss, as it clearly took a number of years for me to heal. What matters is that you wake up in the morning and thank God for the freedom that is coming, because surely, it will come. Don't lose hope. Allow yourself to feel the emotions and take every thought to God. He will not look at you any differently; He adores and values you. He would rather you have some screaming sessions with Him than guard your heart and carry the burden alone. He is the ultimate gentleman; He won't rush you.

Loss is one of those topics a lot of people have an opinion on when it comes to how to fix you. But there is no one book out there that can truly provide healing for each individual who has experienced loss. Everyone processes and deals with loss so differently. Some people grieve for long amounts of time, sometimes sinking into a great depression, stuck in bed, drowning in a sea of sadness. Others process through laughter, surrounding themselves with people and trying to make everyone think they're okay. Some do the opposite and push everyone away. Still others will act as if they're not effected at all, and you're left questioning if they even realize what happened. But one thing I know is that it's okay to not be okay. It's okay to not immediately know how to talk about what you're working through. It's okay to ask questions of God, to lay it all out there: the sadness, the anger, the hurt, and the confusion. It's okay to let laughter back in. It's okay. God totally gets that there is a process for each individual. My process began when I performed my first dance. It's been a constant uphill trek, but don't put limits on yourself or your timeline, and definitely don't put limits on God.

When I stopped limiting myself and seeing myself as just a label, "amputee," I started being able to live. I wanted God to know that I was willing to pursue anything He sent my way. I knew that I was meant to be sent. On my twenty-eighth birthday I determined that I was done allowing fear to drive my decisions—

then I had to determine every day to act on that. I didn't want to allow fear to continue to get in the way of my ministry, my purpose. Fear was a constant battle in my past (fun fact: it still is!), and I had even turned down some incredible job opportunities, too afraid I'd mess up or get fired because I was new in my skill. Though I haven't gone too deeply into this yet, the past couple of years I have studied makeup artistry and special Fx with the desire of working in the movie industry.

However, upon my graduation from Cinema Makeup School in Los Angeles in January 2020, the Covid pandemic happened and everything was put on hold. The few jobs that I had lined up were suddenly postponed or canceled all together. I found that I was actually relieved because I wouldn't have to worry about the potential of failing. But on the morning of my birthday, I decided enough was enough! Although I knew that things in the makeup industry would be on hold until the lockdown ended, that didn't mean I couldn't put my best foot forward and do some work to prepare for when things did open back up. I worked on my website, was active on social media, and did small, safe jobs here and there. I started to feel more confident about putting myself out there. I was so glad I chose to not let my fears keep me from developing a career I am passionate about.

There was still one thing, though, that had me scared for a long time: writing down my story. Since I'm not a writer, it's not like I actually know what I am doing, so the thought of people reading something I spent so much time preparing is incredibly intimidating. But in this season of having downtime from makeup artistry, I knew it was time—time to invest in this book. Unfortunately, I didn't even know how to start! Then just like that, Cristy reached out to me, feeling a spark ignited in her to help me not only start this book but finish it. I was so afraid of putting out a book full of fluff, but Cristy was not afraid. She knew that God had spoken to me about writing this book back when I was twenty-four, but that I had been battling fear and doubt that I could do it. In June 2020, she took matters into her own hands and came up with an agenda and an outline to get us started! A week after she put the agenda together, I had finished the first chapter; that's when Jaina jumped on board to help with the editing. I couldn't have done this without them and their pursuit of God. They were a huge game changer in helping me get focused and stop living in fear of the unknown. Just remember:

Things that matter are scary!

CHAPTER ELEVEN

I CAME, I SAW, I CONQUERED

I am happy to say that even before my twenty-eighth birthday declaration, I did conquer a *few* fears. One thing that had scared me greatly was the idea of swimming. Luckily, I was never a big fan of swimming before I lost my leg, so in a way it wasn't a huge deal. But when you haven't done something in years, it's funny how you can really begin to crave it. So, when I was living in Florida briefly a couple of years ago, a friend who had a beautiful pool invited me over for a weekend getaway. At first I was terrified not only to get in the pool, but to have her family see "Fat Louie." It made me feel very vulnerable, and I struggled with trusting many people with such a thing. But she didn't make a fuss about it at all and soon we both jumped into the pool. She handed me a pool noodle to float on but after a few minutes of floating around

I wanted to see what I could still do. I did a solid doggy paddle that would have made Michael Phelps proud. Granted, all I ever did with two legs was a basic doggy paddle, and I think my form has improved since then.

Before we knew it, my friend and I were laughing so hard as we did handstands and forward and backward underwater spins, *and* I opened my eyes underwater for the first time *ever*. We also lost all control over our laughter after she had gotten out to get a drink of water and returned to see me swimming backward. She thought my *one* leg looked like I had a mermaid fin and she blurted out, "You look so majestic!" I never thought of myself as majestic, but in the water, I did kind of feel that way. We jumped out of the pool after a good two hours, and I went to bed that night feeling an overwhelming urge to cry, but a good cry. I was honored and relieved that swimming was something I was still able to do.

Another fear I had to tackle was hiking. Not only do I have a phobia of spiders (and pretty much any creepy crawler), but not knowing if I would have the endurance for a long hike, or if the trail would trip me up at some point, really scared me. I remember the first hike I went on as an amputee was a very light hike in the Shenandoah Mountains in Virginia. It was a very basic trail and I was pretty fit at the time, as it was during the season that I was dancing frequently. But this past year while I was living in California (a whole story to be told, so stay tuned), my sister and I visited Yosemite National Park. We had no idea what to expect trail wise. In the first five minutes of hiking, we had to go up a huge incline, and I must have looked ridiculous trying to swing my leg around to make it up the hill. But sometimes you just have to own it. The trail was not the easiest, but I did it! I was able to enjoy it and see the huge redwood trees I had heard so much about from my mom.

There was one shaky moment where my prosthetic started to loosen because the trail was making us both very hot and sweaty. After a while it was really hurting so my sister had to help me duck inside one of the huge redwoods and adjust it. Always an adventure. I had to laugh when we made it through the entire five-hour hike, my car in view, only for me to sprain my ankle in the home stretch. I tripped in a hole even after my sister had warned me about it! I had looked directly at it, noted it, and still managed to step directly into it. Yup. I sprained my ankle good. I could not believe that after finishing a challenging five-hour hike, my car was right in front of me and *that's* when I injured myself! As much as I wish it hadn't happened at all, I couldn't have been more thankful that it wasn't three miles back as we were descending the mountain and that Jessica was able to help me quickly hobble to my car.

Another amazing hiking adventure happened in California. My sister wanted to see the "Hollywood" sign, which I had not yet seen, so we decided to make the supposedly short walk up the Hollywood hillside to see it. We parked our car and began what I thought was going to be a short, maybe one-hour, hike. Mind you, I thought this was going to be such a quick trip that I was still wearing my church clothes and shoes. What a fool. We had stopped at Starbucks on our way, so, drinks in hand, we were just marching along. We passed a group of people taking photos and realized that just across from us was a pack of coyotes. They were literally so close that you just needed to walk over a ditch and up a small hill to reach them. We decided if no one else seemed concerned, we weren't going to be either. So eventually, we were forty-five minutes in and I started to feel exhausted. We passed a guy who could clearly see how tired I was, and he said, "You guys are so close! Just a little further!"

Long story short, it was not "just a little further"; it was more like a whole hour and a half further and we were losing daylight. Every time we came to a turn, we assumed the sign was right around the bend. But it never was. It turned out that we had taken the longest path possible to get to the sign—literally, the longest path we could have taken! We did eventually reach the sign, but my prosthetic was badly in need of adjustment, and we still had the entire hike back to the car. Our journey back was actually terrifying. We both stand firmly on the belief that we were being stalked by something the entire trip down the hill. It was most likely a mountain lion, as there were signs everywhere warning people not to be out past dark, since there was a recent sighting in the area. We were both afraid and crying by the time we descended the last big hill. Other people descending were passing us the whole time, probably thinking we were insane—crying and fearing for our lives.

When we reached the area right before the parking lot, where the coyotes had been, Jessica and I both laughed out of nervous exhaustion, wondering if we were going to die at the mouths of coyotes, just feet from my car. It was pitch black at this point, and our imaginations were running wild. So Jessica brought up the idea of singing loudly to keep any predators at bay, with the backup being my pepper spray and our phone flashlight. So I began singing "Firework" by Katy Perry, and after the first chorus, Jessica said, "We are in a life-or-death situation and the song you pick is a *secular* song?" We burst out laughing and Jessica broke out with a good ol' Christian song, "Holy, Holy,

Holy." Needless to say, we survived the trek and laughed until we cried all the way home to our comfy beds.

TRUSTING GOD'S PLAN

Now that I have mentioned living in California, I would love to expand on that because it was truly a God-ordained miracle and a pivotal moment in my life. It also is yet another example of having to overcome my fears and trust that God had a bigger plan than I could even imagine. I have always had a love for travel, and knowing that travel would be part of my job as a makeup artist was a plus. Of all the things I have been afraid of, traveling has never been one of them. My heart and prayer for the past couple of years has been, "Lord, send me. I will go," and wow, has He sent me. Here's a little backstory of how this all came to be.

When *Lord of the Rings: The Fellowship of the Ring* first came out, this girl was a super fan. Yes, you can call me nerdy; I accept that. My brother Michael loves to say that I was obsessed and possessive of my love for *Lord of the Rings*, meaning that when other people said they liked it, I had to make sure they knew that I liked it just a little bit more. Thinking about that time in my life makes me cringe and recoil (because he isn't wrong). However, even with all the cringing that thirteen-year-old me brought to the table, *Lord of the Rings* is what sparked my passion to be a makeup artist. I was just a kid, with other dreams of course at that time, but I was in utter awe of how there was so much beauty in the elves and was completely inspired by the prosthetic work on the Orcs and Uruk-hai. In that very moment, I wanted to know the process of how the artists brought them to life; I wanted to be a part of creating that beautiful world. It was so believable, I totally could have seen an Orc driving in the car beside us as we went out to run errands. To my dismay, I never did see that Orc. But that is what being a makeup artist meant to me—being able to bring to life a vision, a world unlike any we have seen, and make it real to the viewer.

I also love that a film isn't just about the actors or the director; it's about a team and how well the team works together to create the overall vision. When I watch a movie, I get lost in the art, and sometimes I completely miss what is going on in the plot line. Once my parents recognized the fire within me and saw that I was willing to put the hard work in, we discussed the option of pursuing schooling for makeup artistry. So I attended an amazing school in Florida, but the program ended up not covering special Fx to the extent that I needed. The Fx teacher there mentioned that Cinema Makeup School in Los Angeles was an absolute must if I was really serious about taking my skill to the next level. I desired to pursue the school but, due to my current finances, decided that there was no way I could do it. So, I took a job as an assistant makeup artist with hopes of saving for school.

However, through that job, I learned a huge lesson that not everyone has your best interest in mind. The job ended up defeating me as an artist, beating down my self-esteem, and overall stifling my joy. I was repeatedly informed that I was not skilled enough to be an artist and was placed behind a desk to work administration, being told that this was where I was needed. I put my dream of going to LA completely on hold. Not even on hold, but completely out of the picture. I had moved my entire life out of Virginia for this job, thinking it would help me pursue my dream of film, only to be placed behind a desk doing busy work and being told I was nowhere ready for artistry jobs. One day I had an awful chat with my boss, who restated that I was not ready to be on her artistry team and that she needed my main focus to be in the office. Then, while working late that night, I was yelled at by a client who had an issue with her payment plan. I wasn't even in charge of payment plans, but I was the only admin there that evening and was therefore the punching bag. When she left, I sank into my chair and gazed into the nothingness before me, feeling completely numb and confused as to why I was there. I had felt so much peace about taking this job, and I had really covered it in prayer. Door after door had appeared to have opened. But here I was, feeling utterly defeated. I was heartbroken.

As I sat in silence in my little office, one of the instructors who worked there approached me. She told me that she had heard everything and was sorry that that had happened. Then in her classic "tough-love" attitude, she poured into me with conviction and passion. She asked, "What on earth are you doing here? Didn't you want to work in film? Why are you not in Atlanta like we had discussed? You are too talented, too needed in this industry, to be sitting behind a desk waiting for your big moment. What are you waiting for?" That's when I told her about my dream of going to Cinema Makeup School and finishing my education so I could really pursue the beauty and special Fx world. Without skipping a beat she said, "So why are you not already in your car on your way to LA?" I laughed and said, "Well, the school is thirty thousand dollars, let alone the living expenses. There is just no way I can afford it." She quickly replied, "Aren't there loans out there?"

By the end of the night, she had brought me back to life. She may not have known it, but I was hearing God speak through her. I was feeling totally myself again, knowing that I did have a purpose in the industry and I knew God had a plan for me. I didn't need to take the manipulation I was experiencing through that job anymore.

GOD'S INCREDIBLE PROVISION

The next step was filling my parents in. I was so afraid of telling them how awful it had all been, and that after only two months, I felt it was time to leave and pursue more schooling. Shockingly (but really not, because GOD), they were in complete agreement with me and ready to figure out this next step. Actually, almost everyone I talked to felt that I was meant to leave and pursue more schooling. There were the few who didn't understand and thought I should at least give the job a year, but not everyone is going to see God in the move. That is why it is *your* leap of faith, not theirs.

I gave my two-weeks' notice, and in that span of time, I was able to afford placing a deposit for a class that was going to start in June 2019, only three months away. Also in that short time, I met an amazing friend, Michelle. She was taking classes at my place of work and we would often talk during breaks. When she found out I would be attending a school in California, without hesitation she said that she had a home in Woodland Hills, an hour from Cinema Makeup School. Since it was unoccupied while she was in Florida, she offered it to me rent-free for the duration I would need it. I was in shock. I could not believe she was offering this when she barely knew me! Later she told me that she felt God impressing her to offer her home to me. Michelle will never fully know the impact she has had on my story, and that through her taking a chance on me, a stranger, she was helping to fulfill God's story for me. Her family, who lived near her home in California, was a tangible, visible gift from God. I was honored to be entrusted with a beautiful home and to be able to have been a part, and continue to be a part, of their lives.

When my two weeks were over, I headed back to Virginia to begin the process of transplanting my life across the United States. After arriving at home, everything seemed like a blur as things had to move really fast. Because I was now out of work, I was unable to apply for a loan myself, so it fell to my parents. I was so grateful they believed in me so much that they were willing to take out a loan to help me. I was also scared because I knew that it would be a lot of money and that my dad would have to deal with the weight of the loan. But he told me over and over that he felt sure it would be something he could handle.

Applying for the loan was the most confusing and bizarre experience ever. We were told that it had been approved, only to be informed we needed to send in more paperwork. When we sent in the requested documents, we were told that it was basically approved but they needed signatures from their higher ups. Yet we then received a call requesting more documentation. It was a repeated cycle of this. But then a week before I was supposed to leave for California, my dad walked into my room and said, "Guess who is going to California?" and I burst out crying. I was so happy to hear that the loan had finally been approved and that I was going to get to pursue this dream.

The last thing I was awaiting was a confirmation from Michelle that everything was still good to go for the date we would be arriving. Even though the dates had been discussed, I hadn't received a response to the last text I had sent her. But I wasn't concerned. I felt at peace. My parents felt at peace. I realize I say this a lot. Before I moved for my job, I met a pastor and his wife who became like mentors to me. As I talked with them on FaceTime one day, he said something to me that I found so profound: "When you can't hear God, follow the peace." We so often forget that God doesn't speak to us in just one way. One way I have found Him is in the sense of peace. It's not just a calm, it is actual Holy Spirit–given peace. That's how I know. My prayer had been that if the Lord said go, then I would go. I felt Him saying, "Take the leap. Trust Me."

Then just two days before I was set to leave for California, my dad got a call from the bank saying they needed *more* documents from him! We were all devastated and confused, as we had been told that the loan had been approved. I looked to my parents to show me how to respond. Shockingly, they just continued helping me get my car ready for the trip. They felt confident that God would provide the financial support, even if we ended up not being approved for the loan. If this had been the year before, there would have been no way my dad would be sending me across the country, especially not knowing where the money would come from. But he felt an unquestionable peace, and I knew that for my dad to feel a confidence in the unknown was a big deal. So, I trusted. We packed up my car, Jaina and Cristy tagging along for the ride, and the three of us left at 5 a.m. that fine June morning. We had a whole trip planned to get the full experience. Our first stop was in Branson, Missouri, to see Cori, who was performing in a Sight & Sound Theatre production and had gotten us tickets.

The second day we were in Branson, however, things started to appear as if they were falling apart. I hadn't heard back from Michelle regarding the last-minute details, like meeting her mom for the house keys, and was starting to feel concerned, as we would be arriving in California in just three days. She did end up getting back to me expressing that she was a little panicked. There had been a miscommunication with her family and her cousin was living in the house. After an hour of going back and forth with Michelle, as well as her aunt, we concluded that I would live with her aunt for a month or so until her cousin moved out. I was feeling conflicted. While I was grateful that they had graciously provided a place for me to stay, the girls and I would now need to stay in a hotel during the week they were with me, which was an unexpected financial burden. Once I got off the phone, I let Jaina and Cristy know I would cover the hotel cost. They were pretty upset, so I decided to not deal with that issue and instead make another phone call to my bank. During the call, I found out the loan had officially been denied.

What. Was. Happening? All in one day? We were halfway across the country, with everything falling apart, and I had dragged Jaina and Cristy along with me for the ride. The tension was high, the conversation was negative, and the girls were understandably upset. They couldn't believe I hadn't had these things finalized before we left. But the last time I had talked with Michelle, the house was in order; and regarding the loan, my parents had not been concerned. I felt with everything in me that I should keep pushing forward and *trust*. After many tears and conversations that just went in circles, not really getting us anywhere, I told my friends I needed to step out for a little bit.

I headed to the closest Starbucks and called my house. My dad picked up and I asked if Mom was available. To this day, I cannot remember why he never got her on the phone, but I ended up talking with my dad the whole time. I truly believe that God knew I needed my dad in that moment. As I cried in confusion and hurt, I asked my dad if we should turn around and come home. His response was, "Nope. You're going to California. God is going to provide, and I have no doubt that He is orchestrating great things for you through all of this confusion." He also said, "How many times does God have to prove Himself? He has already moved so greatly in your life, don't start doubting Him now."

I dried my tired eyes and thanked him, and then said goodbye. I'm sure that if I had spoken to my mom, she would have given amazing advice. But because I spoke to my dad, the man who has said no to many things due to financial limitations, I was able to hear his confidence. He believed that we were stepping out in God's will and not making an irrational decision. Tension was still high with my friends, but it was because they loved me and wanted to make sure I wasn't walking into a potentially awful situation. What I learned from this experience is that people may challenge and question something that you feel is from God, but it's simply because they did not hear what God spoke to you.

So when trials pop up, which they will, you may have people say, "Maybe this isn't God?" "Maybe this was your own will all along." "Humble yourself and consider that you've made poor decisions." You may even be asked, as I was, "How can you believe God opened these doors when clearly all the doors are looking shut?" But again, others don't know what God has spoken *to you*, what He has impressed on your heart. Because of that, you then have to be willing to extend grace to those who question you, and not surrender your calling because of their words. In the end it is between you and God. When He says go, you go.

That very same night I received a phone call from Michelle letting me know that her cousin was able to work everything out and move out much earlier than expected. My friends and I would need to get a hotel for only two nights! Things immediately were turning around. When God opens a door, even when it appears to be closing, His will cannot be stopped. Remember this.

FINDING MY CONFIDENCE

The week I spent with Jaina and Cristy ended up being a relaxing, wonderful, and healing time. But there was also a tug of emotions as the days were counting down until they had to get on their flight and I would be alone in California, not knowing a single soul. I had lived on my own before and thrived, but here I was so far away from everyone, and I was already starting to feel the isolation. The day came when I dropped them off at the airport, and as we were saying our goodbyes I was being honked at to move my car. When they walked into the terminal, I immediately called my mom. The sense of being alone fell on me swift and heavy and I cried expressing the loss I was feeling. She reminded me that there will be seasons when we feel alone, but that we never truly are. Our heavenly Father is a constant companion and friend. I often think about this verse when I start to feel unsure or afraid of the next steps:

> Be strong and courageous. Do not be afraid or terrified because of them, for the LORD your God goes with you; he will never leave you nor forsake you.
>
> (Deuteronomy 31:6, NIV)

I pulled into the driveway of what would be my home for the next eight months and I took it all in. I felt a sudden, overwhelming confidence that this was going to be a good season, that it had been a hard ride getting there but it would be worth it. Those eight months would be life-changing for me in so many ways. I would be trained under some of the most talented and skilled artists in the industry. I would meet amazing fellow artists and friends whom I would forever cherish. I would find my confidence in myself not only as an artist, but as an independent and strong woman. Any fears of living on my own, wondering if I could do it, vanished as I thrived under my own routine and independence. What was even more amazing was that I saw how every event in my life up to that point had just been preparing me for that season in California.

No tear shed, sleepless night, or stressful encounter
is ever in vain.

CHAPTER TWELVE

HAVE COURAGE, AND BE KIND

The eight months that I lived in California was nothing short of a miracle. There are times when we can say, "I really feel like God was intervening for me." Then there are times when there is absolutely no doubt that He is. He had placed me in a beautiful home, rent free, in which the entire family made me feel like one of their own. They lived nearby and would check in on me and make sure I was adjusting well. They also invited me to join in on family dinners with them occasionally. I experienced two earthquakes while I was there and both times I received a text or call asking if I was all right. I apparently did not know what to do during an earthquake (since I had been through only one in my entire life), but they were quick to give me the correct safety points. They were like my second family. Blessing #1.

Blessing #2 was my classmates. Bonds were formed quickly and there was absolutely no bad blood. We didn't think anything was out of the norm until instructors began praising us for all getting along so well and for not creating any drama. There had apparently been a pretty consistent flow of students who didn't blend, and some even had outright feuds. But I loved my fellow classmates, and I was honored to get to see us all grow together as artists. I knew that God had opened the door for me to attend this class. When I put my deposit down, there were only two spots left, and I almost opted for a later date. But I am so glad I didn't attend the later class, because the bonds created helped me grow closer to the person and artist I wanted to be. One thing that I really loved about my classmates was that we all genuinely wanted to see each other succeed. We would cheer each other on, grab coffee for anyone who was having an off day, and really pour encouragement into each other. These people truly had my back, making me feel protected and looked out for. Being so far from my family, it was good to know that I had people I could rely on.

Continuing on the blessing train, next up is the insane fact that not only was I able to afford groceries and any other needs that popped up while out in "The Valley," but my dad never missed a single payment to the school. You know the financial struggles we have faced in the past; yet somehow the money was there every single month. I am beyond amazed that we made our last school payment just this past June, even in the midst of the hardships that Covid-19 brought. That is blessing #3!

Now, there were days that I questioned whether I had made the right decision in attending Cinema Makeup School and moving all the way across the country. As soon as the thought would come, the reminder would hit me that God had made this all happen, orchestrating every detail. From the chat with the instructor, to my friend Michelle offering her home, to my dad not even batting an eye about the school cost. My heavenly Father was not going to let me doubt that He had indeed orchestrated the entire thing. The #BlessUps did not end there. He was sending an outpouring into my life.

A SENSE OF DREAD

Yet it amazes me that even with all the good God was doing in my life, I felt an overwhelming sense, almost a panic, that there was bad lurking just around the corner. I would call my dad and say, "I am just waiting for the other shoe to drop…" I feel like this is so common in Christians today. We can't seem to bask in His gracious outpour. We feel undeserving of the blessing and therefore react with fear, anxiously expecting something negative. We may feel overwhelmed by the blessings and act as if we are ready for them to halt and our life to go back to "normal." What if we acknowledged the blessings, praised God for His goodness, and received the outpour with open arms instead of curling up in the fetal position expecting the absolute worst right around the corner? In 2 Corinthians 9:8 Paul writes:

> And God is able to make all grace [every favor and earthly blessing] come in abundance to you, so that you may always [under all circumstances, regardless of the need] have complete sufficiency in everything [being completely self-sufficient in Him], and have an abundance for every good work and act of charity. (AMP)

I like the Amplified version of this verse because it really zeroes in on the point. We are God's children, and He finds great pleasure in providing for us. I had forgotten for a long time that He isn't just the King of kings, He's also my Father and my friend. As much as my earthly dad has poured into me, loved me, and given me all that he possibly could, how much more does my heavenly Father want to adorn me? This can be a very humbling thing to realize. When you stop seeing Him as nothing but a rule maker and a God who brings down some serious wrath, and you start seeing Him as the loving Father and friend that He truly is, a whole new world is opened up before you.

Once I stopped questioning why God was being so good to me, I was able to start pouring more into those around me. I was the only Christian among my friends at school. What I initially felt as dread, as I thought persecution would be a constant, actually turned to excitement. I had prayed earlier in the year that the Lord would use me as a bright light. We are meant to be sent to dark places; after all, if light just stays where other light is, how is the darkness ever going to get a taste? There I was, in a completely new world, feeling singled out as a Christian. But I was not afraid. Every day on my ninety-minute drive into the city for school (LA traffic was no joke), I would pray that the Lord would help me to know when to speak up and when to be quiet. I had a nasty habit of getting defensive when I felt an injustice was being served or my faith was being mocked, and I just knew that that wasn't going to be of any benefit here.

I also prayed that Jesus would help me to have courage and be kind (a quote from the new *Cinderella* movie, which I love, though what has become my life motto came from Scripture first: Joshua 1:9; Ephesians 4:32). Day after day, I would pray this prayer. Once at school, I would remain calm, by the grace of God, as people talked poorly about Christianity (Chick-fil-A was always a huge topic), but I would hold my tongue and process before I reacted. You may be thinking that I should have said something to defend Christianity in a non-confrontational way. But I distinctly felt Jesus telling me to show them His love through my actions and not through my words. This. Is. Huge. I cannot overemphasize this. There will definitely be times for speaking up, no doubt about that, but don't take for granted the times when it is important to first build the relationship, and lead by actions, not words.

I loved my friends in California and wanted to show them what being a Christian was really about. They expressed that the only Christians they had interacted with were very loud in proclaiming that they were going to hell, and that they often associate Christians with hypocrites because they would quote a lot of Scripture but then act in the opposite way. I am not saying to never speak up, but that I wanted to extend kindness and love toward my friends first, before I went into depth about my faith. They had experienced a lot of condemnation from people confessing to believe in the God who offers grace and mercy. My friends knew very soon into the relationship that I was a Christian, but I made sure my actions reflected my faith even more so than my words. I knew they were watching to see if my actions lined up with what I said I believed.

Words. Words mean so little nowadays. What do your actions express? What do your actions say about what you believe and would die for? There were times when something really harsh would be said about my God, and I would desire to defend Him, but then I would feel a sudden restraint to hold my tongue. There was a reassurance that He can defend Himself, but what He asked of me in that moment was to love those who hated Him so much and show them that they were cherished. That they were loved. Through the eight months I was there, my friendships grew to the point that my friends knew where I stood, even politically, yet they didn't fight with me about my views. They respected me because I had shown them respect. I was going to show them what my God was really about—not just through words but through actions.

As my classes were coming to an end, I had been praying about whether I should stay in California or head back to the East Coast to pursue my career. A few instructors had expressed to us that to be successful in the industry we *needed* to stay in Los Angeles. But I just couldn't rest in that. I remembered what the pastor and his wife had told me, about following the peace, and in all honesty, I felt a peace that I should move back to the East Coast. The crazy thing was that as I prayed and my graduation approached, I heard more and more people talking about Georgia. The film industry was thriving there. Even instructors started telling me that they felt Atlanta was the place to reside and that jobs would be easier to come by. So after some time, I knew that's where I would go.

The plan was to leave California after graduation, attend my brother Michael's wedding in April, and then figure out the move to Atlanta. But—as it did for everyone in 2020—life came to a screeching halt. I was nervous on the trip back across the United States as the uncertainty and panic arose, but I made it home safely and would be able to ride out the worst of it with my family instead of alone in California.

As my family quarantined, I struggled with the sudden wealth of time I had on my hands. I had just gone through months of classes Monday through Friday, 8:30 a.m. to 5 p.m., constant going, constant homework, constant routine. What weighed on me most at home was having no routine. I thrived on a schedule, yet here I was—no classes to attend, no coffee dates with friends, no work. Just stillness. I panicked, thinking I wasn't being productive enough, guilt-tripping myself for not creating amazing art and posting on social media, or studying my numerous notes from class. I felt ashamed of myself. But then…the craziest thing happened. I grew thankful. Thankful for this downtime. Thankful for the rest. I had just been on a rollercoaster and had had very little time for myself, and here I was able to have all the time in the world to focus on recouping. I was able to process everything that had just happened in my life and reassess the next moves. I allowed myself to stay up a little later, to sleep in, to relax. What I needed was to let myself rest and take the time to mentally prepare for the next season.

With everything being postponed to later in the year, when June rolled around, that is when this book began to form. I am so thankful for the time I got to rest my brain. I would need it fully functioning to be able to recall years of memories and to have the patience to sit down and write my story! I want to make sure that nothing important goes unsaid. I believe that what God intends for this book is exactly what it will be and I only need to rely on Him to finish it. So let's finish it.

PEACE TO STAY

After praying numerous times, "Lord, send me and I will go," I realized I had to be okay also praying, "Give me peace to stay when You say to stay." I had desired Atlanta, and was willing to do everything in my power to get there, but as doors kept closing, I began to feel an uneasiness with moving out there. Then, out of nowhere, I started getting jobs here in Virginia—really fun and creative jobs. I had fought staying in Virginia because I felt like there wasn't anything here for me career-wise. It is funny how we can be so sure we don't want something, only to have God show us how incredible that thing can be. I had a good friend reach out to ask if I was still planning on moving to Atlanta. I told him that I was currently giving Virginia some more of my time. He then proceeded to excitedly shout, *"Don't move!"* He told me he was working on his own film project right here in Virginia and asked me to be a part of the team, serving as head of the makeup department. We set up a meeting to discuss his vision, and I shed tears as I realized that his dream aligned so perfectly with mine. I suddenly knew why God had closed doors in Georgia. I still have that traveler's heart, and I think God is going to use that when the time is right. But I have realized it is so much better to rejoice where God has you than to fight Him to get you into the next season.

So often we don't understand God's timing, and then when events come to pass we tend to feel quite foolish in our angst-ridden humanity. Don't place shame on yourself, but learn from those moments. I had to realize that the prayer isn't always, "Send me"; sometimes it's, "Help me to be content staying." I had to trust that even though I wasn't doing the work I originally thought I would be doing, God was still bringing incredible projects my way through different photographers in the area. If I had moved to Georgia as I had planned to, I would never have found my feral kitty, Shiva, who was living in my parent's garage. During the months of home quarantine, I was able to go out every day and earn her trust (she is now a very content, indoor snuggle bug). If I had moved when I had wanted to, I would not have had some amazing breakthroughs with my dear friends and been able to work through some seriously needed healing. Because I stayed instead of running to the next thing, I was able to really commit to my fitness journey and get myself back to a healthy place. I was able to change my relationship with food and value my body for the temple of God that it is. I poured myself into following a workout routine and, through the help of my accountability partners (Cristy, Casi and Jaina), I have lost twenty-five pounds. It is now a mission of mine to help other amputees modify their workouts so they don't feel defeated and intimidated. Being an amputee is hard, but there is always a modification. You are more than the label placed on you; you can do so much more than you even know.

If I'd gone to Georgia when I wanted to, I would not have reconnected with an old friend from my childhood and been given the chance to start an incredible new relationship. This man had been fifteen minutes away since we were kids, but it took a pandemic for us to reconnect. I also would not have been able to work so heavily on this book. If I had had any control in telling God what I wanted Him to do, I would not be about to embark on an actual dream come true: to work with a team of fellow believers who have an incredible vision to impact Hollywood.

I am so thankful that I serve a loving Lord who knows what is best for me, because He is the author of my story. Every step, every moment, every trial, He had it perfectly arranged to make me into the woman I am today. Every single adventure, every person I came into contact with—it all was for a reason. He created me with a purpose. Each day has been perfectly orchestrated by

His hand. He gave me strength when I felt too weak to stand, and He was gracious to help me to process through my pain. He truly held me close in my darkest hour. My God took a tragedy and brought such a beautiful and full life out of it. What's even crazier is...

This is just the beginning.

I remain confident of this:
I will see the goodness of the LORD
in the land of the living.
Wait for the LORD;
be strong and take heart
and wait for the LORD.

(Psalm 27:13,14, NIV)

ACKNOWLEDGMENTS

To say that this book was my own doing or took minimum effort, would be a total farce. This was a journey, something I could not have done on my own. God knew I needed a strong army of people not only to be prayed up to fight the battles at hand (and there were many that were faced in writing my story), but also to help me remember things that my mind had tucked away due to trauma. This book, though my "baby," has many aunts and uncles that can't go unmentioned.

First and foremost, I have to thank my Lord and Savior, because without Him, my story would have been completely different. I know, with everything inside me, that He has been so gracious and kind to me. Even in my darkest moments, when I blamed Him for my pain, He never left my side. He gets all the glory and the credit for my story. I owe Him all of my gratitude for writing this book, bringing it out of me, and using my hands to type what He desired this book to be.

My four amazing siblings: Thank you for the laughs, for bringing humor back into my life in my darkest hour. Thank you for loving me when I was wallowing in self-pity and wasn't the nicest person to be around, for being a shoulder to cry on in my grief, and for believing that this book would happen in the right timing. You guys are my life. I am so thankful that I get to call each of you my blood.

Cristy Briggs and Jaina Jacobs: For years you both heard my excuses for not writing a book, but your passion and drive served to fuel my excitement! God used you both to light the fire in me to finally get this book going, and He used you to finish it. Thank you for the hours sacrificed to help me edit and remember events that occurred, and for encouraging me when writer's block arose. This book may be my "baby," but without a doubt it is your "stepchild." Thank you for dreaming this book up and seeing it come to life, even before I did.

Suzanne McGhee and Helena Petherson: You were both a huge part in my story then and now. You have both grown into amazing women of God, reflecting Him in your daily lives and marriages. I look up to you so much, and this book wouldn't exist without the memories you gave me. Laughter truly is healing medicine and I can't get enough of it with you two. Suzanne, thank you for all the times you cleaned up my vomit! Little did you know, I was just preparing you for motherhood.

Sarah Worman-Connell: Sarah, you took a broken bird, fixed her wings, and gave her the courage to dance again. You never gave up on me, even through those restless nights trying to choreograph for a one-legged dancer, and you made me feel like I was flying. The laughter at every dance meeting filled me with such joy, teaching me the difference between just being happy and being truly joyful. Thank you, Sarah, for opening up your home to hours of practice, tears, frustration, and growth.

Christine Kearns, "my sister from another mister": Thank you for being my #1 fan in life and treasuring me as your own flesh and blood. You invested into my dreams of being a makeup artist, freely offering business advice and financial wisdom. You saw my loss not as a defeat but as something I would overcome, and you never once gave up on me. I will never be able to thank you enough for those late-night pep talks. Forever my sister, forever my friend.

Cally Henrichs: You are such a gifted author and a treasure of a friend. Every time you had a word from God, you shared it freely with me. You spoke encouragement into me, pouring so much time into late-night chats filled with my own insecurities. Thank you for your selflessness. Your praise and feedback for this book changed it for the better. Your wisdom goes far beyond your age.

Toviyah Troobnick: You've been so supportive, from early writer's block to last-day editing, and you pushed me to finish when I would have rather been reading in the park with you. Tovi, knowing that you were right there, available, really was exactly what I needed in this process. Outside of my family, you were the first person I told about my book being published; that's how much you mean to me. I am so thankful for you, 3000.

Emily McKinney: Thank you, my "boo boo twin," for putting together the benefit dance, a night that forever changed my life. I don't think I will ever be able to thank you enough for believing not only that God would use me in great ways, but that I was capable of more than I was believing myself to be. I am so thankful that you have stayed in my life, in my story, and that we are #foreverfriends.

Angela Donadio: Who would have thought that the sixteen-year-old you cast as Belle at a summer camp would be under your mentorship to this day? God has made you a recurring character in my story, and I couldn't be happier about that. It was an honor to serve as your makeup artist for your book cover on *Astounded* and to have you as my agent and friend on *Held*. I am truly "Astounded" at the life we have walked through. Always and forever.

Casi Briggs: What have we not been through? I cannot picture my life without you. Thank you for loving me at my worst, pushing me toward my best, and supporting me in my many endeavors. You are so wise, Casi, and so strong. You encourage me to grow thick skin, love people when it's hard, and not give up when the going gets rough. Thank you for using your photography skills on the cover of this book; you never stop amazing me with your gift.

My parents, James and Jillana Eadie: Thank you for raising me in the way that I should go. I learned through watching your example. Thank you for always pushing me to be my best self and reminding me, even in my worst moments, of who God has called me to be. You taught me that my story is not my own, that everything we do in this life is to fulfill our biggest purpose—to glorify God. Dad, your words changed my heart that night in the hospital. Mom, your prayers molded my heart into what it is today.

Suzi Wooldridge: Thank you for welcoming me into the Bridge-Logos family! You saw something in this new writer that I couldn't see. I cannot thank you enough for opening that initial email and taking a shot on me. I'm so excited to take this journey with you.

I wish I could write in great detail an acknowledgment of every single person who has had an impact on my journey, but the list would never end! There are so many people (you know who you are) who poured into me and helped me to grow into the woman I am today. For that, I am so grateful and will never be able to thank you all enough. I love you all very deeply. I am who I am today because of you.

AUTHOR BIO

Melissa Eadie is an LA-trained Makeup and Special Fx artist with quite the story to be told. Formerly an aspiring dancer, she is a two-time cancer survivor and above-the-knee amputee—all before her twenties. She believes all ashes can be redeemed into a beautiful story and is passionate about helping those dealing with great loss, whatever shape or form, to process through their grief and healing. A spunky, young cat mom to Miss Shiva Danielle Halpert, she loves to travel to new places and intends to see as much of this world as possible. Connect with Melissa at:

mellydoeslife.com
Instagram: @MellyDoesLife
Facebook: Melly Does Life

ASTOUNDED
Angela Donadio

Some days, real life is more outrageous than fiction. But sometimes, everyday moments are unexpected miracles. Craving a few minutes to step away from schedules and stress? Take a deep breath. *Astounded* is the reprieve you need. Angela Donadio shares raw, personal stories and shows us how to keep our eyes peeled for the miracle hidden in life's messy moments. Because sometimes, when we least expect it, God breathes on a situation and leaves us astounded. As a mom, pastor's wife, musician, adventure junkie and author, Angela understands the roles women carry and the unique pressures they face.

www.angeladonadio.com

ISBN: 978-1-61036-253-5

BRIDGE
LOGOS

FEARLESS
Angela Donadio

What do Jochebed, Rahab, Abigail, the woman at the well, the woman with the issue of blood, and Priscilla have in common? Find your fearlessness in their stories.

This 6-session Bible study will help you to:

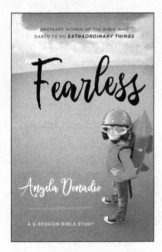

Stand Up / Develop God-confidence to step into your unique calling.

Stand Out / Seize God-moments to make culture-shaping choices.

Stand Strong/ Embrace God-sized dreams to become a catalyst for change.

Readers will find their fearless in the inspiring stories of ordinary women of the Bible who dared to do extraordinary things.

www.angeladonadio.com

ISBN: 978-1-61036-401-0

LET THERE BE JOY
Carol McLeod

"Let There Be Joy!" is a 25-day Christmas devotional that will enable the reader to navigate the busy-ness, the joy and the meaning that solely belongs to this miraculous season. Each day of this December journey presents either a true story that reflects the richness of the Christmas season or teaches a riveting lesson from the treasury of Christmas scriptures. Some days the reader will laugh ... other days the reader will weep ... and hopefully, every day of this Yuletide devotional, the reader will be challenged to embrace the eternal message and meaning of the season that causes the world to stop in awestruck wonder. In addition to the daily devotional readings, each day also presents Bible reading suggestions as well as the opportunity for practical and personal application.

ISBN: 9781610362054

BEAUTY FROM ASHES
Donna Sparks

In a transparent and powerful manner, the author reveals how the Lord took her from the ashes of a life devastated by failed relationships and destructive behavior to bring her into a beautiful and powerful relationship with Him. The author encourages others to allow the Lord to do the same for them.

Donna Sparks is an Assemblies of God evangelist who travels widely to speak at women's conferences and retreats. She lives in Tennessee.

www.story-of-grace.com

www.facebook.com/
donnasparksministries/

www.facebook.com/
AuthorDonnaSparks/

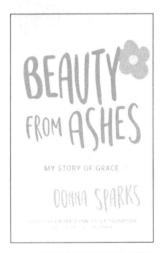

ISBN: 978-1-61036-252-8

FINDING JOY WHEN LIFE IS OUT OF FOCUS

Angela Donadio

We all walk through seasons when joy plays an unwelcome game of hide and seek. This in-depth, verse-by-verse study will help you choose contentment regardless of circumstance, transform faulty thought patterns through the truth of God's Word, and persevere when life is unraveling.

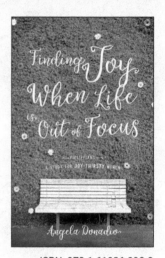

Filled with personal testimony and encouragement, this is an ideal companion for group or personal study.

Angela Donadio is an international speaker, recording artist, and advocate for deprived pastors' wives and children in Africa.

www.angeladonadio.com

ISBN: 978-1-61036-993-0